MW00629758

HOMESTEAD
⤜⟫ FLORIDA ⟫⤛

HOMESTEAD
❧ FLORIDA ❧
FROM RAILROAD BOOM TO SONIC BOOM

SETH H. BRAMSON
AND BOB JENSEN

THE
History
PRESS

Published by The History Press
Charleston, SC 29403
www.historypress.net

Front cover, top: Courtesy Chris Green.
Back cover, bottom: Courtesy Miami-Dade County Parks.

Unless otherwise credited, all images are from the collections of the authors.

First published 2013

ISBN 9781540222251

Library of Congress CIP data applied for.

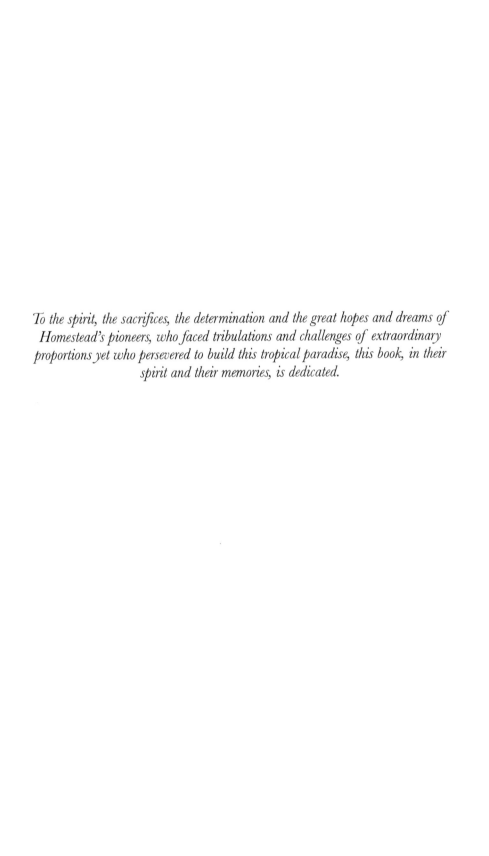

To the spirit, the sacrifices, the determination and the great hopes and dreams of Homestead's pioneers, who faced tribulations and challenges of extraordinary proportions yet who persevered to build this tropical paradise, this book, in their spirit and their memories, is dedicated.

CONTENTS

FOREWORD

The history of Homestead is a combination of pioneer grit, fortitude and optimism that together played a vital role in the history and growth of South Florida. Although pioneers first arrived in the late 1880s, followed by railway workers, families and early businesses, it was in 1913 that Homestead was transformed from an outpost of railway workers into an official community of men and women who were determined to build a town composed of schools, churches, hospitals and commerce.

This book salutes not only those early families but also the succeeding generations of families who have contributed to Homestead's growth over the past one hundred years. Their contributions have helped to make Homestead thrive with rich cultural diversity and creative energy, emerging into the growing and vibrant city we see today.

We hope you will enjoy the historical photographs of people and places that were part of the early story of Homestead. The stories are fascinating and at times heartbreaking as natural and economic disasters repeatedly struck the area. The strength and endurance of this South Florida town as the decades unfold are all about the people you will meet—some familiar names, and others perhaps not previously known to you. Regrettably, limited pages caused us to have to leave out many wonderful stories, events and people as we strove to find a cross-section to represent the tapestry of those who have passed on and those who celebrate our centennial this year. With that said, a rich history becomes known in the coming pages from a perspective of Homestead as viewed by two skilled authors, each covering two separate and challenging periods of growth from Homestead's early development from wilderness to prosperous community, its reemergence from devastation to the thriving city we enjoy today and the threads that bind the periods together.

—YVONNE KNOWLES, CHAIRWOMAN
Homestead Historic Preservation Board

ACKNOWLEDGEMENTS

In considering the preparation of a book celebrating the centennial of a great city, the second incorporated municipality in then Dade and now Miami-Dade County, the Homestead City Council, with the concurrence of the city manager, the Centennial Committee and the Historic Preservation Board of the City felt and believed that the book was meant to be and should be "a two-man (-person) job" and, after proper consideration and deliberation, selected your authors as the people who would write that history.

However, in writing a book on the history of any entity, the author or authors recognize and understand that, while they (in this case, "we") are doing the actual writing, very little could have come to fruition without the wholehearted help, support and assistance of no few people, groups, clubs and organizations.

Before noting and naming those who enabled the authors to complete this several-years-in-the-making (from conception to completion) task by providing materials such as photographs, postcards, booklets, brochures, documents, athletic programs, yearbooks and other material, as well as their reminiscences and recollections, it should be clearly stated that this book could not have been written and published without the total support of the three city-based groups noted in the first three paragraphs below.

Mayor Steven C. Bateman, Vice Mayor Jon Burgess, Councilwoman Patricia Fairclough-McCormick, Councilman Elvis R. Maldonado, Councilman Stephen R. Shelley, Councilwoman Judy Waldman and Councilman Jimmie L. Williams III, upon and with the recommendation of City Manager George Gretsas, voted unanimously to make this book possible by providing the necessary funding.

The City's Centennial Steering Committee, named by the Council, includes Chairwoman Yvonne Knowles, Vice Chairman Timothy L. Craig, Ruth Campbell, Kametra Driver, Steve Losner, Kevin Myles and Maycol "Mike" Enriquez. The committee, appointed in April and May of 2012, worked for months preparing and bringing to fruition various events related to the centennial and their input to the council was instrumental in support of a 100th-anniversary book.

Members of the Historic Preservation Board, also Council appointed, include Chairwoman Yvonne C. Knowles, Vice Chairman Dr. Dennis Ross and board members Luis M. Avila, Katherine Fleming, Susie Peterson Randolph and Clara Waterman Powell. They not only worked closely with the Centennial Steering Committee but were also advocates of a Homestead centennial history being published from the time the idea was first proposed and presented. Suffice to say, your co-authors are grateful not only to the Council, the Steering Committee and the Historic Preservation Board but to the following, who shared so much Homestead history with us.

A very special thank-you goes to Khaleah Evelyn, who served as assigned administrative staff person to the Centennial Steering committee and was responsible for coordinating the administrative side of the Centennial projects as they related to City approvals, contracts, attorney oversight and more. Khaleah was and is invaluable to all that the committee has done and is doing, and everybody involved in this project is very appreciative of all her tireless work.

Retired army lieutenant colonel Charlotte (Charlie) Hudson not only edited a large portion of the book but also was always available for consultation and assistance and was never too busy to answer questions or be of help. Larry Diehl; Carl Schumacher; George Grunwell; noted Homestead and Miami historian, author and postcard collector Larry Wiggins; Ruth Campbell, director of the Historic Homestead Town Hall Museum; Nancy McLean Coppola; Tri-Rail locomotive engineer Richard Beall; photographers Tim Jones and Michael Downey; Howard Salus; WLRN's Ted Grossman; Jack Seitlin; Bill Losner; and Steve Losner all contributed immeasurably with inputs and ideas. Retired Miami-Dade police captain Paul Mallard regaled us with endless stories of Homestead and its people.

Immeasurable kudos must go to Yvonne Knowles, who is named above. Yvonne was an absolute "sparkplug" in support of this project and maintained that support from start to finish, and "we couldn't a done it without her!"

The *South Dade News Leader* and its continuing coverage of the community for almost one hundred years deserves special recognition. Peter Schnebly, of Schnebly Redland's Winery and Brewery, and Joe Reyes, director of sales and marketing of the winery, kindly supplied several fine photographs, as did Jimmy Accursio of the Capri Restaurant. Rob Burr, who contributes so much to Greater Miami in the form of his civic involvement, sent a number of excellent images for our use.

From the City of Homestead, Debbie Moore, in the Procurement and Contracts Division, City Clerk Elizabeth Sewell and Public Information Officer Begone Cazalis were there to help with and answer every request while Travis Glasford of the Phichol Williams Community Center was nothing but helpful in providing information regarding Homestead's early African American settlers.

Chief of Police Alexander E. Rolle Jr. and Police Department Executive Assistant Carmen White welcomed us warmly and provided much information on the department and its operations. Ruth Campbell, who is named above, spent a great deal of time with us at the museum, detailing much of the city's history.

Florida City's city clerk Jennifer Evelyn unhesitatingly provided much information on and about her city and Mayor Otis Wallace, and to all of them we extend our sincere thanks.

The "first ladies" in our lives, Meda Jensen and Myrna Bramson, must not go unremarked, for it was with their unequivocal backing and support that we were able to persevere tirelessly to see this great project through to completion, and we both want them to know how much they—and their presences—mean to us.

As with any history, every effort was made to seek out all pertinent information within the purview of this tome and to meet and/or speak with anybody who could provide information and assistance. If, unintentionally, any individual or group has been omitted from these acknowledgements, our apologies are given in advance along with the promise that, if the omission is brought to our attention, we will endeavor to include those names in future editions.

Chapter 1

A TOWN BETWEEN THE RAILROAD
AND THE FARMS

H omestead and Florida City have rich but relatively short histories
because South Florida was among the last areas in the country to be
settled. The first twenty years in the area were filled with major events that
led to incorporation and growth.

The area east of Krome Avenue was opened to homesteading in 1898
and the area west of Krome in 1900. By 1902, several families had settled
in the area north of what is now Homestead. Henry Flagler, owner of the
Florida East Coast Railway and former Standard Oil founding executive,
had extended the FEC Railway into Miami in 1896. He further extended
the FEC into the village of Cutler (area now around the Charles Deering
Estate) in order to move fruits and vegetables out of that area. Cutler was the
closest place where early homesteaders went for supplies and where they sent
their produce for shipment by boat to Miami for further shipment by train
or ship. Later, in 1903, the FEC completed a survey under the supervision
of William J. Krome to determine whether the better route to Key West was
via Cape Sable to Big Pine Key or directly south from Homestead to Turtle
Harbor on Key Largo. William J. Krome went on to be the chief construction
engineer for the extension to Key West, decided to make Homestead his
home, purchased land and became a leading figure in agriculture.

Earliest known photo of Homestead's Florida East Coast Railway Station. Completed in August 1904, it is now part of the Florida City Florida Pioneer Museum.

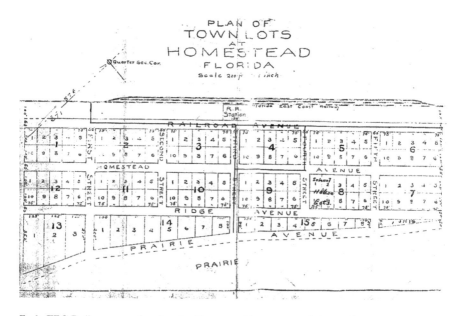

Early FEC Railway map showing the Homestead layout east of the tracks.

First Buildings Are Constructed

William A. King, the FEC section foreman, moved his work camp to Homestead in late 1903 and began construction of the FEC station and the homes for the station agent and the section foreman.

The station was constructed on the west side of what is now Flagler Avenue at about Second Street. Two houses on the south side of Flagler later adjoined the two-story building built by Max Losner to house the Dixie Drug Store at 129 South Flagler Avenue. The FEC buildings, completed in August 1904, were of durable Dade County pine. (As a note, Hurricane Andrew destroyed Homestead station in August 1992, and its new site in Florida City is behind the station agent's house, which still stands.) They have been moved to 826 North Krome Avenue in Florida City for the Florida Pioneer Museum. A replica of the Homestead station was constructed after the hurricane.

In June 1904, the FEC had laid out the town that sprouted twenty-eight miles south of Miami where the tracks stopped. Early survey maps needed to designate the end of the tracks as a destination, so the surveyors labeled it "Homestead Country." Indeed, the first reference to the "homestead country" in records of the Florida Pioneer Museum Association is in a *Miami Metropolis* July 4, 1902 article that reported on the Florida East Coast Railway survey underway to choose a route from Miami to the lower tip of the peninsula. The area south of Cutler was referred to as the "homestead country," the area in which homesteading was taking place. Between 1902 and 1904, newspaper articles on the area south of Cutler were often titled: "Homestead Country." A popular story goes that when construction was underway on the extension of the tracks from Miami south, workers made reference to the area in directing boxcars south by writing "homestead country" on the cars with chalk.

Had Henry Flagler been in charge, the city of Homestead could easily have been named the city of Ingraham or Ingrahamville. A *Miami Metropolis* November 27, 1903 newspaper article reported:

> The terminal has not been named but it will be in what is known as the homestead country in section 13, township 56, range 38, six miles east of the end of the pine land on the mainland of the State, or about thirty miles southwest of Miami. Mr. Ingraham has secured 600 acres of land for this purpose from the Government to be used for buildings, yards and other terminal purposes. Mr. Ingraham is delighted with the terminal site. He says

that it overlooks an immense prairie, over which the sails of craft on the bay can be seen toward the east while toward the south can be seen the mangrove swamps on the edges of the waters of Card Sound and the Bay of Florida.

Two letters received from the St. Augustine Historical Society clearly show the modesty of FEC Railway third vice-president James E. Ingraham. In a January 4, 1904 letter to FEC vice-president and general manager J.R. Parrott, J.E. Ingraham thanked their boss Henry Flagler for proposing that the "terminus" in the homestead country be named Ingraham, but he believed "it would hardly be fair to take all the glory of it to myself, and I therefore suggest that the place be named 'Homestead.' It is the homestead country, and the name has an attractive sort of a sound that may help bring people to it and establish it as a center. I shall be glad to have your further advice in the matter before we put the name on our map for publication."

J.E. Parrott responded on January 15, 1904, "Referring to above; your suggestion of 'HOMESTEAD' as name for present terminus of the Cutler Extension meets with Mr. Flagler's approval, and you may therefore arrange to place same on your printed matter."

As the FEC's third vice-president for lands and industrial enterprises, Ingraham did continue to play an important role developing South Miami-Dade County. When the Florida Federation of Women's Clubs (FFWC) was working to establish Florida's first state park at Royal Palm Hammock, he facilitated Mrs. Henry Flagler's donation of 960 acres of land. Later, he and local county commissioner W.J. Tweedell assisted the Woman's Club of Homestead's involvement in the building of the road to the park.

Years later, the Woman's Club of Homestead helped see to it that the road from Miami to the park became Ingraham Highway and that Railroad Avenue in Homestead be renamed for Henry Flagler.

FLORIDA EAST COAST RAILWAY EXTENSION TO KEY WEST

Henry Flagler clearly envisioned extending his railway from the mainland over the Keys to Key West. Official historian of the FEC Seth Bramson attributes the beginning of the extension to the hiring of Joseph C. Meredith as his chief construction engineer in 1904. He announced his intentions to bring his railway to Key West to its leading citizens in January 1905.

Railroad (now Flagler) Avenue sometime between 1910 and 1912 from a postcard. The buildings to the right of the station are the first commercial buildings.

Homestead did not play a major role in the construction. A *Miami Metropolis* article of August 1906 reported, "A vast amount of material for the F.E.C. Railway extension building is now being transported by rail to the Homestead section, the most of the material at present being intended to complete the track from the present terminus to Jewfish Creek, where the line leaves the mainland for the Keys." A very early Florida Pioneer Museum postcard shows railroad wooden ties stacked high along the FEC tracks south of the depot. Most of the construction supplies were later shipped by water. The important commodity of fresh water was shipped to the Keys using cypress wood tanks on flat cars.

Homestead's biggest gain from the extension was the families who settled here after construction was completed. Three very notable FEC men were William J. Krome, the man who was the chief project engineer for the completion of construction; J.D. Redd, who became chair of the Dade County Commission; and S.E. "Sid" Livingston, who was Homestead's first clerk and tax assessor, school board member, mayor and then postmaster. Interestingly, Krome devoted most of his remaining life to South Dade horticulture and became a world horticultural authority.

The first citizen of the new town not associated with the railroad, however, was William D. Horne, who purchased two lots south of the railway station

The William J. Krome home place at Krome and Avocado Drive, shown circa 1910, was long called "Krome Corner."

from the Model Land Company, Henry Flagler's landholding company. He built a store with living quarters on the second floor and rented lodging to occasional visitors. In December 1904, his wife, Ida Campbell Horne, arrived by train with their household possessions. Next, Charles McMinn, a bachelor, homesteaded a tract that ran from Krome Avenue to McMinn Road. Then David Sullivan and his sons David, George and Homer came from Cutler and lived at Richard Road and Avocado Drive. The parents of Mrs. Horne, Thomas A. and Elizabeth Campbell, took up a homestead on the west side of Krome around Eighth Street (Campbell Drive) in the summer of 1906, and later the same year, Horne's brother-in-law, R.E. Caves, homesteaded the northwest corner of Avocado Drive and Tennessee Road. Horne sold his store to Caves to devote his energies to his farming, his packinghouse and his real estate interests. Horne was "Mister First" in Homestead: first merchant, first packinghouse owner, first postmaster and first bank president.

SCHOOLS ARE BUILT

Homestead had sixteen or seventeen children by the fall of 1907, qualifying them for a Dade County school. The FEC Model Land Company supplied a lot at Northeast First Road and Second Drive; the school board furnished the lumber; and W.D. Horne, Charles McMinn, R.E. Caves and James Wesley Campbell constructed the one-room building, later adding a second classroom and using the building until 1913. If the school was provided a name, it was not recorded in available records.

The cemetery was located next to the new school, which Dr. John B. Tower considered to be a health risk. Dr. Tower, who had arrived in 1910

The two FEC Bungalows on Railroad Street (now Flagler Avenue). Constructed in 1904, they housed the station agent and the track foreman.

from Topeka, Kansas, had become Homestead's first doctor after he was called upon to assist with an outbreak of typhoid fever. In order to ensure the school could remain, the Model Land Company donated land on Old Dixie Highway in Naranja for a new cemetery and citizen volunteers transferred the remains on special "cemetery work days." Establishing the cemetery was a real community project with a lead role taken by the Pioneer Guild, a women's social group that met in its own Guild Hall at the corner of Redland Road and Bauer Drive. The Guild Hall still stands as the Redland Grocery.

Churches Are Next

The first church that was officially recorded as established and built in Homestead was First Baptist Church, organized on September 5, 1909, with founding members Reverend H.H. Sturgis, Mr. and Mrs. W.D. Horne, Mr. and Mrs. T.A. Campbell and Mrs. S.E. Livingston. Mr. Livingston was a charter member of the Methodist Episcopal Church South that was also organized in 1909 by the Reverend F.L. Glennen with Livingston and Mrs.

C.W. Little, among other charter members. The church was a part of a South Dade circuit composed of Homestead Methodist Episcopal South, Silver Palm and Perrine with the parsonage at Silver Palm. The Sunday school was organized in 1913.

A Methodist Episcopal Church North was organized in 1914. More than a decade later, Homestead became known all over the United States in 1929 when the two Homestead Methodist Episcopal churches became the first in the nation to unite since the 1844 split of the churches over the issues of administration and slavery. The original church bell donated to the new ME Church South in 1914 by Leonard Mowry now sits in front of the United Methodist Church at Krome and Seventh Street.

BUSINESS DISTRICTS: BANK OF HOMESTEAD

The first business district was developed along Flagler Avenue south and east of the FEC Railway tracks. If one thing spurred the development of Krome Avenue as the main commercial artery, it was construction of the Bank of Homestead at North Krome and Mowry in 1912 by contractor N.E. Lewis. W.D. Horne was the founding president, and officers were Horne, president; Thomas Brewer, vice-president; H.R. Pridgen, cashier; and directors were Horne, Thomas Brewer, R.E. Caves, D.M. Roberts and A.C. Horne.

Homestead Mercantile Company, chartered in 1912, constructed its first building directly north of the bank and doubled its size with an addition to the north in 1914. Horne was president (eighty shares); Henry Brooker Sr., vice-president (sixty shares); and S.E. Livingston, secretary and treasurer (sixty shares). Their attorney, J.L. Billingsley, assisted the incorporators of the Town of Homestead at their first meeting. Homestead's first elevator was installed in that building November 1912.

A second story was added to the Bank of Homestead in 1917. Until recently, the state-chartered Bank of Homestead was thought to be an independent, locally owned bank, but it was probably controlled by William S. Witham, affectionately called "Uncle Willie" in prosperous times. From the 1912 beginning, he probably owned controlling interest and was responsible for hiring senior bank officers who seemed to move from one Witham System bank to another. The Witham System, also known as the Bankers Trust Company of Atlanta, Georgia, was said to have 160 banks scattered around Georgia, Florida, New York and New Jersey.

Auto Park Place, Homestead, Fla.

The FEC Depot provided a parking lot for the growing population of automobiles.

In July 1916, bank vice-president Thomas Brewer, his wife and Mr. and Mrs. J.M. Bauer drove to Atlantic City, New Jersey, for the convention of the "Witham System of Bankers." That same year it was reported that Witham was heavily involved in buying Dade County real estate. The next year, a report stated that the Bank of Homestead "was regarded by the Witham System as being one of the most promising and prosperous to be found in the country sections of the State of Florida."

Moving ahead in the sequence of events, in March 1920 when the bank voted to increase capital by $10,000 after a prosperous year, it was understated that the Witham System would continue to own a block of stock. The Witham System had its own "expert examiners"—auditors. The bank was enlarged dramatically in 1925 and also went over $1 million in total assets.

When the Bank of Homestead failed in June 1927, was reorganized twice and finally closed for good in 1931, taking local depositors' funds (this was before funds were federally insured), the local directors took full responsibility, not blaming their problems on the Witham System.

FIRST NEWSPAPER

Homestead's first newspaper, the *South Florida Banner*, was established March 15, 1912, by Reverend J.A. Kahl, who helped found the Methodist Episcopal Church North and was instrumental in the incorporation of Homestead as a town. Police protection, a better school and the authority to enforce sanitation laws were the incentives for the citizens of Homestead to incorporate. Increased taxes and the possibility that saloons would be set up in Homestead were arguments spoken of by opponents.

INCORPORATION OF HOMESTEAD

The December 13, 1912 edition of the *South Florida Banner* contains the first mention of plans to incorporate. A boxed notice on the front page was headlined: "MASS MEETING, NEXT TUESDAY EVENING AT 7 O'CLOCK AT THE SCHOOL HOUSE. Every man in Homestead [*this was before women's suffrage*] is invited to be present at the mass Meeting to be held at the School House next Tuesday evening, December 17, for the purpose of discussing the practicability of incorporating Homestead. Let nothing prevent you from attending this meeting as it is of utmost importance to Homestead. Everybody come prepared to do something for your town."

Reverend Kahl's front-page editorial strongly encouraged all voters to attend, and he defended against the arguments of increased taxation and the possibility of getting saloons in Homestead. He added that incorporation would provide the authority "to enforce laws favorable to sanitation" and the push needed for a better school and better equipment for the more than one hundred students expected in 1913.

About forty male citizens attended the December 17 planning meeting according to the December 20, 1912 *South Florida Banner*, and all but one voted in favor of incorporation. Kahl acted as temporary chairman and A.W. Chapman as temporary secretary. Miami and Fort Lauderdale city attorney "Mr. Billingsley" was present and gave legal advice. The chair appointed a committee of Dr. J.E. Miller, J.U. Free and S.E. Livingston who prepared the required legal notice that later appeared in the *Banner* on December 20 and 27. Another argument for incorporation given by the *Banner* declared, "We need police protection. The winter brings a great many strangers here who remain only for the packing season and experience has taught us that we need more police power than we have had in the past."

On February 7, 1913, the *Banner* published the minutes of the second meeting, held on January 27 at 7:30 p.m. at the schoolhouse as the official notice had announced. Reverend Kahl and A.W. Chapman were elected chairman and secretary again. Attorney H.P. Branning attended and "guided the proceeding along legal lines." He also donated his services, which may be why he attended rather than Mr. Billingsley. The chair read the official notice published in the *Banner* and then after the motion passed, Kahl selected G.M. Budd, R.F. Tatum and J.E. Cochran as a committee to ascertain and report on the qualifications of those present to participate in the voting. The twenty-six qualified electors who responded to the roll call were:

E.L. Brooks
G.M. Budd
F.A. Campbell
J.W. Campbell
W.B. Caves
A.W. Chapman
J.E. Cochran
A.T. Duval
T.E. Evans
J.U. Free
J.A. Kahl
P.D. Lamb
S.E. Livingston
F.S. Loomis
F.N. Martin
W.H. Mathewson
A.J. Miller
L.S. Mowery (Mowry)
J.D. Redd
Charles Sherritt
J.W. Simpson
F.J. Springer
D.R. Sullivan
D.W. Sullivan
R.F. Tatum
W.J. Tweedell

J.D. Redd, one of three
notable FEC men who helped
incorporate Homestead and
served in multiple city and
county public service roles, is
seen in this 1911 photo.

A quorum was present since twenty-five electors constituted a quorum. A motion was made that the vote be taken by show of hands. Objections were made, and the motion was withdrawn with the vote taken by secret ballot. The tellers reported that twenty-one ballots were cast for incorporation and five against. Memories not always being accurate, stories in later years variously have had just one or two nay votes.

The name "Town of Homestead of Dade County, Florida" and a corporate seal were adopted.

The last order of business was electing officials. R.F. Tatum was elected mayor over J.E. Cochran. Aldermen were: W.J. Tweedell, G.M. Budd, J.D. Redd, J.E. Cochran and J.U. Free. Unsuccessful aldermen candidates were: Reverend J.A. Kahl, S.E. Livingston, A.T. Duval, L.S. Mowery (also Mowry) and F.S. Loomis. (In his eightieth decade, Livingston remembered that Mowery and Duval had voted against incorporation, and here we see they ran for alderman at the very same meeting.) Livingston was elected town clerk over W.B. Caves ("Bunny"), who would later fill the clerk's job, and A.W. Chapman. F.J. Springer was elected marshal over A.J. Miller and D.W. Sullivan.

Although called the Board of Aldermen in the minutes of the organizational meeting, their minutes at their very first meeting read:

"First Meeting Town Council Homestead Fla. Feb 3, 1913." Elected officials had signed their oaths of office on January 29. Meeting in the Campbell Brothers Store House, the council took as its first action the election of J.U. Free as president of council for one year. It then voted that W.J. Tweedell, G.M. Budd and Free would serve two-year terms and J.E. Cochran and J.D. Redd one-year terms. Eight ordinances were introduced at that first meeting. It was agreed to post the ordinances on doors and windows of town hall (the former Campbell Brothers Store House) and the "market place" of the Homestead Mercantile Company for four weeks as prescribed by law.

The record of the incorporation proceedings of January 27, 1913, was filed with the Dade County Circuit Court on February 8, 1913.

The Town of Homestead was reincorporated as the City of Homestead in 1923 when the Florida legislature enacted a charter for and created the City of Homestead. At this time, the population of the city had surpassed 2,500, which was the population threshold between towns and cities. It must have been a cause for celebration.

THE DANGER OF FIRE IN HOMESTEAD

The Town of Homestead had no firefighting equipment or even a volunteer fire department. Homestead's first major fire on November 10, 1913, burned down five buildings on what is now Flagler Avenue in downtown Homestead in two hours. The fire began about 2:00 p.m. in the Homestead Inn, now Hotel Redland. The nearby barbershop of John Killinger caught fire next, followed by the new and not yet occupied real estate office of L.A. Love. J.E. Cochrane's house just south of this office also caught fire.

By March 1914, Homestead had purchased a fire engine and planned a volunteer fire department. The new fire engine arrived March 27, 1914, and the hand-drawn pumper was tested at the canal near Detroit, now Florida City. Between six hundred and seven hundred feet of new hose was also purchased. Walter J. Tweedell, who was simultaneously serving as the Dade County commissioner for District Five (the southernmost district), dug wells in multiple locations. The volunteers and a few paid firemen of the newly organized Homestead Volunteer Fire Department provided fire protection until that responsibility was turned over to Miami Dade County after the 1950s.

Many new commercial buildings subsequently opted for masonry construction rather than wood, a practice spreading throughout the United States after having entire downtowns burned to the ground.

In April 1922, fire destroyed the Homestead Growers' Association packinghouse. Although the adjoining fertilizer warehouse of B.W. Morris, also used by Horne and Horton as a packinghouse, was destroyed, the Hector Supply warehouse and Homestead Mercantile Company buildings were saved. The City's primary 1917 American La France Type 40 Triple Pumper fire truck was augmented in March 1924 when the City ordered a new model American La France Type 75 triple compound fire engine. In 1935, the City acquired a 1933 Sentry model centrifugal pumping, hose and chemical truck. The truck, from the Seagrave Company of Columbus, Ohio, was specifically built for sub-tropical service.

Another major fire on March 8, 1940, fueled by forty mile-per-hour winds, required additional equipment from South Miami, Coral Gables and Miami, but the Seminole Theater on North Krome Avenue could not be saved. The fire had begun on the stage half an hour before the show was to start.

FLORIDA CITY INCORPORATES

Twenty-three months and one day after Homestead's decision to incorporate, its neighbor to the south, Detroit, followed suit but with a twist. That town had gotten its name from the former hometown of some of its early settlers: Detroit, Michigan. This no doubt caused problems with the U.S. Mail, and when eligible voters gathered in the town hall on December 28, 1914, they included the issue of a new name: that of Florida City. An interesting note is that Detroit was not an incorporated town, but it had a town hall. Homestead, an incorporated town, had no town hall until 1917. Detroit's town hall was built in 1911 by public subscription, at a cost of $1,000. One incentive for Detroit to incorporate came from continuing talk in Homestead of incorporating its neighbor to the south into the Town of Homestead.

WOMAN'S CLUB OF HOMESTEAD

Homestead and South Miami-Dade's oldest civic organization is the Woman's Club of Homestead. Despite not being able to vote, these women surely knew what needed to be done in the community and how to get it done. Name a significant event in Homestead's history beginning in 1914, and the Woman's Club of Homestead has probably had a role in it. The club ran a free dental clinic for many years, helped with the first and second plantings of palm trees along Krome Avenue and sponsored the application for Royal Palm State Park founder May Mann Jennings to be named one the Great Floridians 2000. (Homesteaders also named were W.H. Krome and Max Losner.) The club was among the first sponsors of local political forums.

The club, formed on September 26, 1914, at the Evans Hotel (now the Hotel Redland), made its first task to outfit the domestic science (home economics) department of the Homestead School. In that busy year, the club also solicited donations of grapefruit, shipped an entire railroad carload to New York, sold it and donated the money to the Red Cross to aid those who suffered from World War I. By July 1915, the club had established a lending library at the Evans Hotel. The lounge at the Hotel Redland is named the Library for that reason.

Other women's clubs were organized in Princeton, Redland and Longview (across the street north of today's Robert is Here produce, fruit and milkshake stand, and the old building still stands).

In actuality, the Woman's Club was probably organized primarily to lead the local efforts in establishing a state park in the Everglades. May Mann Jennings, president of the Florida Federation of Women's Clubs (FFWC), took on the preservation of the Everglades as a major project in 1914. One of her strongest supporters was FFWC conservation chairman Mrs. Kirk Munroe of Coconut Grove. Jennings came to Homestead in August 1915 to speak to members from the Larkins, Longview, Princeton, Redland and Homestead women's clubs. She called on members to make her dream of a state park at Paradise Key–Royal Palm Hammock a reality and solicited attendees' help in pushing the work on the Dade County road to Royal Palm Hammock and Cape Sable. The women of the Homestead Club immediately did so by asking the county to keep convicts working on the road. Member Maisie Tweedell had no problem in getting the requests quickly to the county; her husband was County Commissioner W.J. Tweedell. Although the Florida legislature established Royal Palm State

The Woman's Club of Homestead clubhouse, at the northwest corner of Eighth Avenue and Fourth Street on land donated by Mrs. E.C. Loveland, was constructed in 1923.

Park as the first state park in Florida, it turned down the FFWC request for $1,000 to operate the park. Undaunted, Maisie requested and received the money from Dade County.

In 1916, the FFWC constructed a lodge at Royal Palm State Park on land donated by Mrs. Henry Flagler, widow of the owner of the Florida East Coast Railway, and by the State of Florida. A pavilion, plant house, garage and water tower were constructed later.

When Royal Palm State Park was dedicated on November 23, 1916, more than one thousand people came, arriving by 168 automobiles. Homestead Woman's Club served everyone lunch at the park with a little help from husbands. The state later added another 2,080 acres. Royal Palm State Park was operated by the FFWC from 1915 until December 6, 1947, when the ladies donated their property to the federal government for the establishment of Everglades National Park. A plaque honoring May Mann Jennings as one of the one hundred great Floridians appropriately hangs in the Hotel Redland.

Another club project in 1915 was establishing a reading room or library with two hundred volumes. Many of the libraries around Florida were established by women's clubs, and some are still operated by the clubs. The 1920s saw much activity with the club honoring local school faculty members in 1921 and joining the 1922 Homestead shade tree campaign.

In 1923, the club constructed a clubhouse at 410 Northwest Eighth Avenue on land donated by member Mrs. E.C. Loveland. Opening day of the first Redland Fruit Festival in 1924 was designated Woman's Club Day. In 1925 when the Rotary Club of Homestead received its charter, the Woman's Club hosted the luncheon.

The club obtained use of the triangular piece of land on which the El Toro Taco Restaurant now sits from the FEC to use as a park in 1925 and paid for its landscaping and the laying of sod. The park, most often referred to as Legion Park or Triangle Park, on which El Toro Taco now sits, lasted until 1945 when the City of Homestead declined to purchase it and private interests built a shopping center there.

The club also turned its library over to the City of Homestead in 1926; librarian and club member Lily Lawrence Bow was deputized, given a badge and paid as a Homestead policeman until the 1927 budget contained funds for a librarian.

The Junior Woman's Club of Homestead was formed March 25, 1935. They participated in many subsequent Woman's Club events and efforts as well as initiatives of their own.

When Everglades National Park was established in December 1947, the club gave a reception for out-of-town visitors at the First Presbyterian Sunday School building, now called City Church.

Among their ongoing civic works through the decades, the club helped found the Florida Pioneer Museum in 1962–64 and continues to support it financially to this day.

NEW HOMESTEAD SCHOOLS CONSTRUCTED

The small wooden Homestead School was replaced in March 1914 by a masonry structure of modern design at 151 Northwest Fifth Street. Miami architect August Geiger designed it along the lines of schools in Southern California to provide comfort in pre–air conditioning days using overhangs and large windows for ventilation. The four-room school, with H.E. Alderhold as the first principal, was expanded in 1915 and again in 1917. Neva King Cooper was appointed principal of the elementary school in 1926, and the school was renamed for her in 1934.

Homestead High School, constructed nearby on Northwest Second Avenue in 1921 to alleviate overcrowding and separate it from the elementary school, was the first stand-alone high school and junior high. In 1937, contractor Ralph Moon constructed an addition to the ten-room school. The local district school board consisted of S.A. King, S.E. Livingston and Dr. J.B. Tower. The 1921 faculty included L.C. Bennett, principal; C.R. Daniel, chemistry; Gertrude E. Williams, history; Grace Burwell, domestic science; Mattie Stoval, mathematics; Eleanor Chambliss, English and Latin; Annie Lawton, eighth grade; and Mrs. C.R. Daniel, seventh grade. After South Dade High School was constructed in 1953, the original high school campus became Homestead Middle School.

CHAMBER OF COMMERCE

The Homestead Chamber of Commerce was organized in early July 1915 with twenty-four charter members. Then as now, the chamber worked as a part of a team with the Cities of Homestead and Florida City to make South Dade a better place to do business and raise a family. S.E. "Sid" Livingston was elected president; Dr. J.B. Tower, vice-president; and pioneer banker H.R. Pridgen, secretary-treasurer.

Interestingly, Florida City, previously called Detroit, had established its equivalent of a chamber of commerce: the Detroit Booster Club. It benefited greatly from the support of the Miami Land and Development Company, which owned Detroit and the surrounding area. The company developed, marketed and sold the town off lot by lot and the farm land in ten-acre blocks. The Homestead Chamber of Commerce may have been established in the shadow of the great public relations success of the Detroit Booster Club.

Dr. B.F. Forrest, the first mayor of Florida City, attended the second meeting of the Homestead Chamber of Commerce with "ten of his up-to-date boosters." A medical doctor who was working as a horticulturist, Dr. Forrest declined to accept an important committee chairmanship "as he didn't have the time to devote to the matter." For the third meeting, "a special invite to friends from Florida City, Redland, Naranja, Princeton and other county towns" was extended in the *Homestead Enterprise*. Two of the chamber's initial concerns were the building of the Cape Sable Road and the perceived excessive profits of fertilizer companies.

The chamber reorganized in November 1917 as the South Dade Chamber of Commerce. Two key issues were the action of the Farm

Across from the FEC Depot about 1916. Tatum Real Estate Office was owned by R.F.
Tatum, Homestead's first mayor in 1913. People not identified.

Loan Board in turning down applications for loans from this locality and
organizing a celebration for the formal acceptance of Homestead's first
electric lighting system. Bank of Homestead cashier W.M. Bradley was
elected president, and a regional diversity was achieved with A.L. Hearn
of Silver Palm elected vice-president; Lewis Twyman of Homestead,
secretary; P.L. Carlton of Modello, assistant secretary; and O.B. Parker of
Redland, treasurer.

Two more reorganizations followed in December 1918 and in July 1920.
Henry Flagler's landholding company, the Model Land Company, paid for
the printing of the first known local chamber promotional booklet in May
1921, and thanks to the late Paul Losner, the Florida Pioneer Museum owns
an original booklet.

Throughout the next forty years, the chamber was involved in many business
and municipal projects that benefitted the surrounding communities.

THE 1916–17 CITY COUNCIL TOOK BOLD ACTIONS

Fifty-eight of the sixty-one Town of Homestead registered voters went to the polls on January 13, 1916, in what may have been Homestead's most important election. The 1916 election was also the first election of all town officials for two-year terms instead of one-year terms.

Mayor R.F. Tatum (Russell) was sworn in on January 27 by the Honorable A.H. Love, justice of the peace of the Eighth District of Dade County. The early mayor's main duty was to administer justice in the town court while working closely with the chief of police (or marshal, as he was earlier called).

The town councilmen elected in 1916 who did such an outstanding job of planning for the future of Homestead were J.D. Redd, W.F. Winn, J.E. Cochran, D.H. Flowers, Joe Burton, R.E. Edwards and W.J. Tweedell.

The mayor did not preside at council meetings: this task fell to the council president who was elected by fellow councilmen. The 1916 council unanimously elected Redd president. The important and highly contested committee assignments were also voted on by the entire council. They were:

Finance: J.D. Redd
Sanitary & Electric Light: Joe Burton
Fire Department: W.F. Winn
Police: R.E. Edwards
Streets and Sewer: J.E. Cochran
Public Buildings: D.H. Flowers
Parks and Docks: W.J. Tweedell

Elected town officers were:

Clerk: W.B. (Bunny) Caves
Chief of Police: E.A. Sistrunk
Tax Assessor: A.H. Love

At its February 10, 1916 meeting, the council elected S.E. Livingston as auditor and Robert Glenn as fire chief.

The 1916–17 council was a far-sighted, hardworking group of men who met often and late into the night. A $40,000 bond issue financed several far-reaching projects that influenced the town's growth.

The council built the town hall, awarding the low bid to local contractor J.E. Umphrey. The building on North Krome Avenue, which also housed the police and fire stations, remained in use for its main purpose until 1975. Other projects were street improvements, more land, improving fire protection and installing and equipping a municipal light plant, which the city operates to this date.

On February 6, 1917, the council awarded the contract for the electric light plant to the Gibbs Gas Engine Company for a "turn key" operation, according to the *Homestead Enterprise*. The site selected was known as the "jail lot," Lot No. 11, E.L. Brooks Addition. On March 5, 1917, the council voted to trade this lot to B.M. Duncan for Lots 3 and 4, Nelson's Addition.

The town hall was reported by the *Homestead Enterprise* as nearly completed on August 16, 1917: "The building is large and spacious and meets admirably the requirements for which it was designed, the base being equipped for the fire department, in the rear of which is the jail and the second story for a court room and municipal offices."

Construction on the school grounds (Neva King Cooper School) brought the number of classrooms to twelve, "all on one floor and an auditorium about which they cluster."

In September 1917, the town council authorized the issuance of bonds for the construction of additional sidewalks and curbs. The council accepted the Bank of Homestead's offer to purchase these special improvement bonds and agreed not to dispose of any of them but to keep them in its possession.

On a different note, at the January 17, 1917 Homestead Town Council meeting, a letter was read from the "Honorable Edward Stiling of Florida City in regards to Homestead and Florida City combining and having *one live town*." A meeting held in Florida City on January 27 resulted in a unanimous objection to annexing the Town of Florida City to the Town of Homestead.

The team that led Homestead so successfully during the critical development years was broken up in late 1917. W.H. Sykes (William) was elected by the council to replace W.F. Winn, who had moved away. In a special election on October 16, 1917, S.A. King ran unopposed to replace R.F. Tatum as mayor. King had been defeated by Livingston in a February 10, 1916 Town Council ballot for town auditor.

The 1917 Religion Survey

In 1917, prior to the building of post–World War I churches, Dr. W.J. Barton made a canvass of the town to ascertain the religious inclinations of its inhabitants, with the following results: "Adventists, 7; Christian Science, 1; Baptist, 315; Christian Disciples, 11; Church of God, 4; Catholics, 6; Congregationalists, 7; Christian and Mission Alliance, 2; Episcopalian, 21; I.B.S.A. [*Author's note:* Explanation of this denomination was not provided in the survey.], 2; Lutherans, 8; Mormons, 4; Methodists, 149; Presbyterians, 16; Quakers, 1. Making a total of about 650 white people professing some religion, while a great many refused to state their preference."

As had been previously mentioned, the official records showed that the first churches established in Homestead were First Baptist Church of Homestead and the Methodist Episcopal Church of Homestead in 1909 followed by Sacred Heart Catholic Church and St. John's Episcopal Church, both in 1916. There is reason to believe that the predominantly black St. Paul's Missionary Baptist Church was established as early as 1903, but the physical church by that name was not built until 1948. Dr. W.J. Barton, however, did not address this in his 1917 survey, and so we do not know if he was aware of St. Paul's importance.

Chapter 2

WORLD WAR I, BOOMS, BUSTS AND HURRICANES

WORLD WAR I

While notable events were unfolding locally, war had erupted in Europe and our country's entry into World War I resulted in fifty-five men from Homestead serving in the army and twenty in the navy.

John G. Salley, U.S. Army died in defense of our country, and in 1919, the American Legion Post 43 was named for him. Since World War I records were maintained by race, we know that four members of the black community died in this war defending our country:

Francis, Ephraim, of Perrine—U.S. Army
Nelson, Archie, of Homestead—U.S. Army
Pfleger, Frederick, of Princeton—USMC
Tanner, John Fluckers, of Naranja—U.S. Army

Records of those who served were:
Army Private Albrecht, Alfred C.
Army Sergeant Allen, William R.
Army Private Arnold, Joseph L.
Army Private First Class Atkins, Eddie
Army Private Banks, Pierce
Army Private Bazemore, Winford W.
Army Corporal Biggers, Benjamine L.

Army Wagoner Bow, Douglas M.
Army Private Burden, George F.
Army Private Byrd, John Thomas
Army Chauffeur Camp, Paul Z.
Navy Pharmacist Mate Third Class Chandler, Luther
Army Corporal Crowley, Ernest Zuma
Navy Fireman First Class Dixon, Leo Percy
Army Sergeant Draper, William E.
Army Private First Class Drayton, Samuel Lee
Army Private Duboise, William C.
Army Sergeant First Class Duncan, Bob M.
Army Private Ewing, William Cornelius
Army Private Fields, Joe
Navy Quartermaster First Class Fuchs, Charles Theodore
Army Corporal Gelling, Robert H.
Army Gossman, Jesse E.
Navy Fireman Second Class Gossman, Walter Charlie
Navy Seaman Second Class Granger, John Carol
Navy Seaman Second Class Hammon, Fred Willingwell
Army Sergeant Hamon, Ray L.
Navy Hospital Apprentice First Class Harris, Thomas Jefferson
Army Private Hearn, John M.
Navy Pharmacist Mate Third Class Hearn, Walter Neal
Navy Yeoman First Class Hearn, William Abner
Army Wagoner Hobbs, Foy B.
Army Private Hobson, Robert C.
Army Private Ingram, Otis D.
Army Private Ivan, Joe
Army Corporal Jackson, Tony
Navy Electrician First Class Radio Johnston, Hugh Maxwell
Army Sergeant Joiner, Burrell L.
Navy Mess Attendant Third Class Kelly, Frank Christopher
Navy Landsman Carpenter Mate Aviation Knighton, Harvey Bevins
Army First Lieutenant Medical Corp Lanier, William Tomlinson
Army Private First Class Little, Floyd L.
Army Sergeant Lowe, George F.
Navy Storekeeper Second Class Mc Clanahan, Howard Samuel
Army Private McCray, Arthur
Army Private First Class Moore, Albert S.

Navy Machinist Mate First Class Morris, Benjamin Warren
Army Private Moser, Ivan E.
Army Private Neeley, Charles H.
Army Private Nelson, Archie
Army Private Nipper, James C.
Navy Chief Machinist Parham, Charles Hooker
Army Sergeant Porter, Hoke
Army Private First Class Reams, Philip D.
Army Wagoner Pride, Henry
Army Private Richardson, George
Army Private Ross, George N.
Army Private Ross, Julius
Army Private First Class Ross, William
Army Private First Class Salley, John G.
Navy Landsman Quartermaster Saunders, William Barnes
Army Corporal Smith, Otis M.
Army Private Snell, David B.
Army Private Soper, Jesse A.
Army Private Straughter, Clyde
Army Private Thompson, Earnest
Army Private Thompson, Edward
Navy Seaman Vann, James Columbus
Navy Fireman Third Class Vihlen, Claus Erick
Navy Seaman Second Class Vihlen, Hugo Cornelious
Army Private First Class Walker, Perry
Navy Mess Attendant Third Class Williams, Mose
Army Private Wim, Thomas O.
Navy Machinist Mate Second Class Woodbury, Edward Richard

Those black men who served and returned were:

Lawyer George Washington Aker of Peters
Charley Ashley of Goulds
Eddie Adkins of Homestead
Pierce Banks of Homestead
Edwin Baptiste of Perrine
Joseph Burney of Goulds
John Thomas Byrd of Homestead
Samuel Leo Drayten of Homestead (*Miami Herald* listed as Drayton)

Wilfred Ferguson of Redland
Joe Fields of Homestead
Moses Griffin of Perrine
Frederick T. Holmes of Princeton
Joe Ivan of Homestead
Tony Jackson of Homestead
Ed Leonard of Goulds
Richard Theodore Lodge of Goulds
John Mabery of Goulds
Fred Mader of Perrine
Hector McCain of Princeton
Arthur McCray of Homestead
John McDonald of Peters
Charles H. Neiley of Homestead
James Simon Philmore of Peters
Hoke Porter of Homestead (*Miami Herald* listed as Poke)
Henry Pride of Homestead
Edward Reid of Princeton
Bert Reynolds of Goulds
George Richardson of Homestead
Tom Roberts of Peters
Arthur Robinson of Goulds
Julius Ross of Homestead
Richard W. Sands of Goulds
Edward M. Simms of Princeton
Russell Singleton of Florida City
Hardy Smith of Goulds

A WINDOW INTO THE BLACK COMMUNITY IN WORLD WAR I

In October 1918, the black community stood up to help "alleviate the sufferings of the sick ones, and have done good work making broths and delicacies which have been greatly needed." The unit was called the Colored Red Cross. This work is the first known example of local Red Cross assistance in local emergency relief. Then in December it was reported, "The ladies of the Colored Red Cross for purposes of the Christmas Roll Call are covering the colored sections of Goulds, Princeton and Homestead." The Roll Call was a drive for funds and for new members.

The black community had organized its own Red Cross unit in May 1918 with Ida Logan as chairman, Georgie Jenkins as vice-chairman, Carrie Batton as secretary and Lizzie Meldeton as treasurer. Members were: Annie Woolford, Mary Thomas, Annie Williams, Eliza Meredith, Laura Abron, Dollie Young, Nellie Colston, Mary Mason, Susie Robinson, Mary Broughton, Annie Jackson, Moselle Zonicle, Masie Watson, Susie Matthews, Luella Curtis, Christina Taylor, Pattie Mills, Alberta Duncan, Pauline Clayton, Mamie Blue, Lila Maxey, Ethel Jones, Frankie Simon and Mrs. Flukes. Mrs. Camp, Mrs. K.K. Horton and Mrs. Tibbets from the South Dade unit were at the organizational meeting to give instructions. The unit was to meet the next Wednesday with Ida Logan. The ladies divided themselves into four teams, and their initial work was on bandages and "foot-sox," supplies that were in great need in France.

This small window into the black community is very rare for the early days of our history since we are so dependent on newspaper reporting, that usually did not cover the black community.

HOMESTEAD'S EARLY HOSPITALS

The first hospital in the South Dade area was a Florida City hospital owned by Florence M. (Mrs. John W.) Hunt. After she came to then Detroit in 1913, Mrs. Hunt started nursing in private homes, taking care of one patient at a time. In 1917, she rented a two-story house in Florida City at First Street and Northwest First Avenue and named it the Florida City Hospital. Two years later, Dr. John Tower convinced her to start a hospital in Homestead located on Palmetto (Fourth) Street and sold her Lot 28, Tower Addition. Mrs. Hunt contracted with Ralph O. Moon to construct the six-room bungalow that opened September 11, 1919. When Mrs. Hunt got too busy, she called on a Miami nurse, Mrs. W.I. Fiske, for help.

Mr. and Mrs. W.I. Fiske then established the Fiske Post Graduate Hospital in 1922 at Northwest Pine (First) Avenue and Campbell Drive. Dr. Smith and nurses Mrs. Fiske and Mrs. Lena Cavender staffed the Post Graduate Hospital, despite Dr. Smith referring to it as a "five-room house made over into a hospital." Dr. A.M. Logan, nurses Mrs. J. Nesbitt and Mrs. Margaret Fox and nurse anesthetist Mrs. Veda Mock later joined them. The correct spelling of the Fiske family name is thought to be "Fisk," although the Fiske spelling predominated. In March 1925, the Rotary Club of Homestead voted to contribute $1,500 to the "new Fiske Hospital," although it never came to pass. In March 1926, the Homestead City Council authorized Dr. J.A. Smith to proceed with plans for a model twenty-two-room hospital that was to be leased to a private institution.

Mrs. Fiske closed the hospital in 1940 when the new James Archer Smith Hospital finally opened. Ironically, she died the same week that the Fiske Post Graduate Hospital was converted to apartments. Hurricane Andrew destroyed that building and the nurses' quarters across the street to the east.

HOMESTEAD GETS A SECOND BANK

Homestead Enterprise publisher-editor A.C. Graw led a group of businessmen who organized the new Citizens Bank of Homestead at a March 24, 1920 meeting. Graw was elected president of the bank and of the board of directors. Vice-presidents were W.J. Carter and S.A. King. Other directors were: I.R. Matthews, E.N Gause (elected cashier as well), E.A. Carter and Paul R. Scott. Reasons given for establishing the Citizen's Bank as a second bank for Homestead were:

1) If the local bank undertook to care for the demands made by builders and owners, it would not be in shape to care for the needs of growers and businessmen generally. This was obviously how the older Bank of Homestead was viewed by the Citizens Bank founders—probably accurately, as it was a part of the Witham System.

2) So many large accounts were carried in Miami by residents of South Dade.

By May 20, 1920, a modern, substantial building was being constructed at North Krome and Miller Street (now First Street Northwest). On October 6, 1920, the first customer, now nameless, deposited $1,000 on a rainy morning.

The end came for Citizen's Bank on July 3, 1926, when it closed its doors at 10:00 a.m. "for reorganization" and did not recover. Depositors' funds were not insured, since this closure preceded the establishment of the Federal Deposit Insurance Corporation in 1933 by Congress. By the end of 1927, depositors had received 55 percent of their deposits back.

BASEBALL STADIUM AND THE CHAMPIONSHIP TEAM OF 1921

In those boom days but before the grave problems of 1926, Homestead's baseball stadium was constructed in 1921 when Homestead had its greatest team, one that was league champion while playing against teams from much larger cities. The baseball field near where Harris Field is now located had a backstop and stands that looked to be covered with chicken wire, and the surface of the playing field was pretty rough. The baseball diamond was identified as a former "landing station for aeroplanes during the war."

Harry O. Hall, star pitcher of the Tomato Growers baseball team and employed at the Seminole Pharmacy, moved his wife and children to Homestead. It was not uncommon for businesses to hire good baseball players to lure them to their hometown teams. Dr. James Archer Smith played second base, and Florida City resident Glenn Summers also pitched, fielded well and was a heavy hitter.

The players enjoyed benefits of being on the team, such as when local engineer A.R. Livingston took the Tomato Growers' photo. After they clinched the title, Mrs. W.H. Cauley, a most enthusiastic fan, treated the team to ice cream and cake at the Seminole Pharmacy. J.W. "Jim" English let team members and their sweethearts (also wives) into the picture show free. This was apparently not something that Jim often did.

Between April and October 1921, the Tomato Growers won thirty-seven and lost just three games. They scored 371 runs and gave up 153. Newly arrived real estate man (and later mayor) H.A. Cameron wrote the sporting editor of the *Brooklyn Eagle* to challenge the winners of the World Series to a series of games to be played in Homestead, winner to take all the gate receipts. No response was noted. Homestead withdrew from the league in April 1922.

POST–WORLD WAR I PROSPERITY

Indeed, the end of World War I and the return of veterans started a period of great prosperity in Homestead and the surrounding area. New construction took off as the veterans gave new vitality to the community. Some even ran for office and won.

March 15, 1925. El Patio Apartments owned by Mr. F.L. Webster, a prominent local builder. Some of his buildings are still in use.

The El Patio Building at 77 West Mowry Street was 56 by 115 feet and housed fourteen apartments that opened onto a courtyard.

The greatest eighteen months in Homestead's history arguably could be from January 1925 to June 1926. Three one-hundred-plus-bed hotels were planned: the five-story Dixie Palm Hotel on North Krome Avenue, the McDonald Hotel on Krome and the Avocado Hotel on Flagler Avenue. A one-thousand-seat theater with a ballroom, a patio cafe, four stores and a filling station was planned for South Krome. Materials arrived, but significant construction never took place on these structures except for the Dixie Palm Hotel on North Krome between Fourteenth and Fifteenth Streets. The first floor of the hotel was constructed before the bottom fell out of the economy. The completed first floor later became the shopping center where Bobbie Jo's Diner is located.

The Redland District Chamber of Commerce acquired land for a right-of-way and convinced the Seaboard Line Railroad to extend its tracks to Homestead. Thus farmers and merchants finally had an alternative to the FEC Railway.

Two large privately owned hospitals were planned. The Fiske Postgraduate Hospital expanded with the help of the Rotary Club of Homestead and Henry Brooker Jr. A major food chain, A&P, opened a store on South Krome Avenue.

The Homestead Building and Loan Association as well as a mortgage investment company were established, and the Bank of Homestead doubled its floor space, creating an interior worthy of any large city bank.

The city expanded from 1.5625 to about 5.0000 square miles, with new boundaries consisting of roughly Avocado Drive to the north, Lucy Street to the south, Redland Road on the west and "Farm Life School Extension Road" on the east. Redland Road was extended from Mowry Street south to Palm Drive in Florida City.

The Homestead Real Estate Board was organized with Joe Burton as president. W.B. Flowers constructed the Flowers Building, and the downtown Hausman Building was also constructed at 123 North Krome Avenue.

The Lions Club, now known as the Redland Lions Club, was formed, and the Homestead Golf and Country Club was set up on Country Club Road as the chamber elected Mrs. Annie Roberts its first woman director. The R.L. Polk Co. published the first and only directory on Homestead until the mid-1950s.

No one anticipated the burst of the real estate bubble, and while the 1926 hurricane was popularly blamed for the bottom falling out of the economy, it only finished the job. Whereas the Great Depression was declared in 1929, South Florida's depression began three years earlier and the very wet 1929

The George W. Hall Cottage, Homestead's first California mission style bungalow, was constructed in 1916 by contractor J.F. Umphrey. He later built the town hall.

hurricane added to the area's misery. Homestead and Miami did not emerge economically until 1941, despite a myriad of federal programs. More on that later.

Efforts of the Chamber

In the chamber's early years of successes, J.D. Redd was among the directors and probably Homestead's best-known elected official. Redd served ten years on the Homestead council, several terms as president. He became a county commissioner for nearly twenty years, twice as chairman. He was chairman of the Dade County Board of Commissioners in 1925–26, a very key period in early Homestead's development.

September 1923 brought another reorganization and adoption of the name Redland District Chamber of Commerce with directors to be elected from these districts: Homestead (six seats), Florida City (three seats) and one each from Redland, Silver Palm, Modello, Naranja, Princeton and Goulds. Income was augmented by a grant from Dade County and allocations from

The first Redland District Fruit Festival took place in 1924, as seen in this photo taken on Krome Avenue. *Courtesy George Fuller Family.*

Burton's Department Store float in the 1924 Redland Fruit Festival. Burton's, a major store for decades, later became Hood's. *Courtesy George Fuller Family.*

Built in March 1924, Homestead's first municipal pool was nicknamed the "filling station pool" because it was behind a filling station. *Courtesy George Fuller Family.*

the "City" of Homestead and the Town of Florida City, based on one mil of the assessed property values. The chamber grew to ninety members.

Unaware of the fragility of the post–World War I prosperity, the chamber built its first building, adjoining old City Hall to the south, in early 1924, and organized the first Redland District Fruit Festival. The 1925 president, Charles T. Fuchs Sr., proudly announced that the chamber had grown to three hundred members.

A lack of funds in the hard times made it difficult to keep the chamber doors open. In 1935, with 102 members, it sought to convince one of five circuses contacted to make Homestead its winter home and later sponsored and organized the dedication of Homestead Municipal Airport in December. In fact, the chamber was involved to at least some degree in most major municipal and regional efforts aimed at economic growth and quality of life.

FIRST HOMESTEAD POLICE CHIEF KILLED

When the push for town incorporation was initiated, one of the issues was the need to have better police protection. That goal was achieved, although with it came the danger that police officers have always faced. People were saddened when Police Chief Charlie D. Bryant was killed in the line of duty in June 1923 while attempting to apprehend William Simmons, reportedly a known bootlegger.

HOMESTEAD'S NOTABLE PHOTOGRAPHERS

The first person to record the visual history of Homestead in an artful way was Carl Turnage of Turnage Studio. Carl came to Homestead in the summer of 1923 with a big reputation as an army aerial and White House and Washington, D.C. photographer. He reportedly traveled with Woodrow Wilson during the presidential campaign and with President Harding in Panama. Carl set up his studio on the second floor of the Horne Building and quickly lived up to his reputation, photographing the people and events of the boom period of 1925–26. Sadly, he committed suicide in July 1927 at the age of thirty-five. Family members say that after the tragedy, his wife angrily entered his studio and ripped up all the photos she could find.

A photographer who made significant contributions from the 1920s through the 1940s was Miami freelance photographer Gleason Waite Romer. He made a photographic record of almost every major personage and event in South Florida and supplemented his income by taking photographs for color picture postcards. This venture brought Romer to South Dade and to Homestead. The Florida Pioneer Museum was permitted to copy some of the negatives of shots of Redland and of Homestead. Jane Fuchs Wilson, daughter of Charles T. Fuchs Jr., generously contributed to the Pioneer Museum, making its South Dade Romer Collection possible.

Maitland Studio was owned and operated by Maitland Davidson across from the police station on the site of the old Triangle Park and later at 310 Washington Avenue. Maitland, a former navy photographer, recorded the visual history of Homestead and South Dade from the mid-1950s to the early 1970s.

As a teenager, Marlow Jacobsen had a keen interest in photography, and his photos of the Florida East Coast Railway, the construction of Homestead Army Air Field and the Homestead Municipal Airport stand out. Marlow served in the navy in World War II as an aerial photographer.

Local photographer Jack Levy grew up in Redland and established a studio in Homestead as a young man. Jack, incredibly talented, distinguished himself by the long period of his work. He was also a community leader as chamber of commerce president, longtime South Dade Country Fair president and as a member of the Florida National Guard.

These great photographers were significantly responsible for the visual history of Homestead and South Dade.

FORMAL SCHOOL FOR BLACK COMMUNITY ESTABLISHED

Local newspapers did not record the event, but oral histories did. A Spellman Seminary graduate from Atlanta, Georgia, Fannie Starr Turner established a school for the black community in 1924. What started with one room dedicated for teaching developed into a school that had a student body of seventy-five to one hundred students, and the curriculum included Latin, algebra, science, art, music and drama. Teachers were recruited from Miami but were expected to live and worship in the community. In a 1990 or 1991 interview with Miami Dade College students Frank Chisholm, Toni Feo and Bobiann Quigley, former kindergarten teacher the late Ernestine Seymore remembered her mother paying twenty-five cents per week for her to attend school and recalled that it was held in a tent. The school later became A.L. Lewis Elementary and then Laura C. Saunders Elementary.

ROTARY CLUB OF HOMESTEAD RECEIVED ITS CHARTER

The Rotary Club of Homestead received its charter in January 1925. Previously it was known as the Luncheon Club. The club set about to help enhance the community, and one of the first projects was to support the Woman's Club of Homestead in beautifying Legion/Triangle Park and the Florida East Coast Railway right of way. As a part of that plan, the Rotarians took on the responsibility for planting the palm trees along Krome Avenue. The Rotarians met for some time at the clubhouse of the Woman's Club. They continue to this day as an active organization, although they do meet at the Capri Restaurant in Florida City rather than at the Woman's Club. Their annual dinner and auction to raise money for scholarships is a highlight that many people look forward to each year.

The 1926 Hurricane

The September 18, 1926 hurricane passed directly over Homestead/Florida City with winds estimated at 150 miles per hour. By some assessments, the economic damage of this storm exceeds all others, and factoring in inflation, it was three times as expensive as Hurricane Andrew because it struck Miami and Coral Gables. The University of Miami chose Hurricanes as its sports team name because of it and the ibis as its mascot because folklore has it that the ibis is the last bird to leave before a hurricane.

Winds downed 120 electric power poles in Homestead as both of the newspapers, the *Homestead Enterprise* and the *Homestead Leader*, lost their roofs and were put out of commission.

On September 20, a two-week power outage was anticipated in the business district since the old power plant on South Flagler was badly damaged. Expectations were that the new one on North Flagler would be back in operation more quickly. Homestead maintained water service by using a fire truck to pump the water into the mains, probably the newer truck—the 1924 American LaFrance Type 75—and that truck is on display in the Old Town Hall Museum today.

The 1926 hurricane damage is visible at Northwest First Street and Krome Avenue. Doc Crow's Seminole Drugstore, which also housed the post office, was next door to the Citizen's Bank Building.

Of two deaths recorded, Mrs. Elmer Shuck was killed when her home in Goulds collapsed. Her baby in her arms was only slightly bruised, and her husband was hospitalized but survived. Fred Schutt, son of W.C. Schutt, Florida City town marshal, was killed in Miami by flying glass.

The back (east) side of the landmark three-story Horne Building, constructed of Denison load-bearing clay blocks, was blown off. Although later demolished in Hurricane Andrew, one of the blocks was saved by the Florida Pioneer Museum.

The Methodist Episcopal Church at First Avenue and Fourth Street lost its steeple, which was replaced with a shorter, less ornate version. The Methodist Episcopal Church South suffered substantial damage, as did most churches in the community. Total storm damages were estimated at $40,000 to $50,000 (in today's dollars, $520,000 to $650,000).

THE 1929 HURRICANE

The September 28, 1929 hurricane had winds measured at 115 to 125 miles per hour with the center of the hurricane passing over Key Largo and the Upper Keys. The countryside was flooded by rains and water from the canals and the bay, although damage to property was confined mostly to businesses. The Homestead Growers Association large steel packinghouse and the corrugated iron packinghouse of the Royal Palm Truckers Association were both nearly destroyed.

The *Homestead Leader*'s Duplex printing press was in four feet of water, yet staff removed the motor, had it repaired and put out the newspaper five days later. They did reduce publication from twice a week to Thursdays only and continued that schedule through at least the end of 1929.

People waded through flooded downtown streets; Ben Flowers and Ben Edwards rowed a boat through the grounds of the El Patio apartment house on West Mowry. The Homestead grammar school was used as a storm shelter, and the Red Cross food relief headquarters moved from the school to City Hall. Once again, Homestead used its fire engines to pump water out of the fish-filled downtown storm sewers onto lots where it drained off.

Gordon W. Ivey, longtime superintendent of the Homestead Power Plant, anticipated restoring power by October 6 since only thirty power poles were downed. All but eleven of the telephone lines of Southern

Homestead Furniture, Redland District Chamber of Commerce and city hall after the 1929 hurricane, which was a very wet one.

Bell's Homestead exchange were knocked out of service, but fifty had been restored within five days.

The Florida East Coast Railway from Florida City to Key West was said to have been hit harder than by any hurricane since 1910. Fourteen miles of track from six miles south of Florida City were destroyed, and the road bed washed away, but eleven days later, mail trains were running between Miami and Key West. Ironically, the well-known construction engineer William J. Krome died at age fifty-two in his home on October 2. Some thought his death was brought on by the hurricane, but friends stated, "He was a man of iron who had little use for sentimentality."

U.S. Congresswoman Ruth Bryan Owens sent a message of sympathy and assurance via the *Homestead Leader*: "I am leaving for Washington tonight, and I am going to scour the departments there for something for the Redland District. I am not sure what is needed most or how best to go after it, but I want you to know—and I wish there was a way to let the people of Homestead, Florida City and other communities in the district know—how completely my heart and mind are filled with their difficulties and how earnestly I want to do all that can be done in their interest."

By the next week, grove owners began resetting the estimated thirty thousand fruit trees blown over. County agricultural agent C.H. Steffani estimated that half of that number could not be reset by their owners. Miami businesspeople raised funds for the Red Cross to hire crews to help, and they started work by October 8. Redland District growers estimated their losses at $1.6 million on investments of $4 million ($208 million and $520 million in 2012 dollars) and asked for federal assistance. Losses by tomato and other vegetable growers were just $47,000.

It is noteworthy that South Dade folks were very self-sufficient and inventive in responding to emergencies and were supported by their Dade County neighbors, both then and now.

First National Bank of Homestead Chartered

Max Losner, a local merchant who moved from Tampa to Homestead in 1923, was planning in 1927 to establish a nationally chartered bank in Homestead. Along with a group of backers, he offered to reorganize the Bank of Homestead after one of its closings, but this offer was not accepted. After some short delays, Max Losner and his backers received the charter for the First National Bank of Homestead in late October 1932. Max Losner had already purchased the Bank of Homestead building, furniture and fixtures, and he opened the new bank on November 1, 1932. In 1935, it joined the Federal Deposit Insurance Corporation (FDIC was established in 1933 and began operations in 1934). The bank led all Dade County banks with a 190 percent increase in deposits two years before Max Losner obtained controlling interest of the bank and was elected president, serving in that position until his death on February 3, 1964.

First National opened a branch at Homestead Army Air Field in 1944 and continued to expand with new branches and supporting many charitable community projects. Paul Losner and William H. "Bill" Losner were both president and board chairman of the bank during their tenures. In 2001, the bank changed its name from First National Bank of Homestead to 1st National Bank of South Florida to reflect the expanded service area.

Chapter 3

THE GREAT DEPRESSION, WORLD WAR II AND NEW AIRPLANES

RECOVERY FROM THE GREAT DEPRESSION

South Florida began suffering its major economic downturn in mid-1926, and notwithstanding attempts to recover agriculture with the introduction of truck crops and crop diversification, it wasn't enough to offset other dire economic realities.

Speaking to the Rotary Club of Homestead in May 1935, Dade County agricultural agent Charles Steffani summarized efforts on the part of the agricultural community to recover from the 1926 hurricane:

> *In 1926, the hurricane destroyed most of the citrus groves and growers began to look for another pay crop to plant until their wind-torn groves came back. By 1928, there were 18,000 acres of tomatoes planted in the district. Cuban and Mexican competition and a general let down in the market cut into this avenue of revenue and many fields were left unpicked because of low prices.*
>
> *Manganese was introduced as an aid to fertilizer in 1929 and with it came the beginning of planting of truck crops, potatoes and broccoli. The growers found that the real "pay lode" was in the diversified planting and by 1930–31 the tomato acreage had declined to 5,000 acres from which 77 (railroad) cars were shipped, while 208 cars of truck crops left the district. Since 1931, the truck crop industry has increased rapidly and for the first time last season corn was shipped from the district by the carload.*

This year more than 20,000 acres of diversified crops were planted. Within the nine-year scope, the packing houses have increased from five to twenty in South Dade from South Miami to Florida City. Canning plants have sprung up over the district to reclaim the ripe fruit which was formerly left to rot in the field and has created an important source of employment. This year nine plants were in operation.

The City of Homestead participated in many federal programs introduced to pull us out of the Great Depression. Local men who worked in these programs often received only a couple days work each week; the number depended on their family size. The programs did provide construction of a municipal swimming pool, Lily Lawrence Bow Library, Homestead Municipal Airport, Homestead Municipal Park, James Archer Smith Hospital and Florida City State Farmers Market; resurvey and re-mapping of the city of Homestead; Civilian Conservation Corps Company 262 Camp on South Krome; repair of public schools; and nursing, art, sewing and swimming lessons.

In actuality, four massive federal construction projects begun just before the outbreak of World War II were what really boosted the economy:

Civilian Conservation Corps Company 262 Camp on South Krome. Men arrived October 30, 1933, as the first passengers to Homestead using the Seaboard Airline Railroad.

The Lily Lawrence Bow Library, a Works Progress Administration project, was dedicated in December 1939 with twenty thousand volumes. Lily Lawrence Bow was Homestead's first librarian.

Florida City State Farmer's Market on May 2, 1957. The building was originally constructed in 1939.

Another WPA project completed in August 1942 was a 130-mile water pipeline project from Homestead to Key West that carried the vital commodity.

Opposite, top: December 1939 photo of Northwest Fourth Street taken by Marion Post Walcott. Buildings are a mix of houses and businesses.

Opposite, bottom: Redland Farm Labor Camp Houses were constructed in 1941 and 1942. Due to segregation laws, a separate camp was constructed for black families.

- The airfield, which became Homestead Army Air Field
- The navy water pipe line from southwest of Florida City to Key West
- The Overseas Highway from Florida City to Key West over the old Florida East Coast Railway right-of-way
- Five hundred units of farmworker housing on Campbell Drive near the base and on U.S. 1

DUAL LIVES FOR THE HOMESTEAD AIR FIELD

Among other efforts, Homestead officials wanted to establish airfield facilities. In 1929 and 1930, Pan Am engineers inspected property on Kings Highway and Country Club Drive west of Homestead as a possible emergency landing site. The most unlikely possibility came in 1934 when an $11 million plan for a combined airfield and seaplane basin was discussed for an area southwest of Florida City as an alternative to expansion of Chapman Field opposed by wealthy neighbors. The astronomical costs kept this project from serious consideration.

Homestead's municipal airport was actually rooted in the 1931 Redland District Chamber of Commerce Aviation Committee. It proposed a temporary runway on the field west of Sixth Avenue on Kings Highway, which commercial planes had been using for sightseeing passenger flights. W.I. Fisk made the proposal, which would have had the field open in time for the Eighth Redland District Fruit Festival in a month's time. George Ranson offered to lease the city a one-hundred-acre tract for an airport east of the FEC tracks on Kings Highway at nominal rental for five years with an option to then buy the tract.

That proposal failed, as did one in July 1931 when S.E. "Sid" Livingston, acting committee chair, received a letter from Henry A. Jencks, International Airports Corporation executive committee chairman, expressing interest in a Homestead location.

In late January 1934, however, the east–west runway of the municipal airport was almost complete and work was to begin soon on the north–south runway. In February 1934, long before the airport dedication, a Pure Oil Company autogiro became the first plane to use the new airport, and a six-place Bellanca followed. In July, a Bellanca, an American-manufactured airplane—sometimes called the Model T Ford of the air—was flown across the Atlantic Ocean. The visits were sponsored by the Seaboard Oil Company, whose local agent was A.J. Campbell.

A big dedication program sponsored by the Redland District Chamber of Commerce was set, and eighteen Army General Headquarters bombers performed for the crowd. The Florida Pioneer Museum postal collection includes a first-day cover mailed via air mail from Homestead annotated, "Homestead Florida AIRPORT DEDICATION December 11, 1935."

Public Works Agency (PWA) had approved a $41,818 grant and loan to the City, and in early January 1936, City Engineer E.L. Hook Jr. began preparing an application for Works Progress Administration (WPA) Project funds to construct a hangar at the south side of the airport where the City had tentatively selected a site.

Homestead Municipal Airport was completed in December 1935. This photo from a card circa 1940s shows four Delta Air Corps Huff-Dalend crop-dusters.

From left to right: South Dade farmer Ernest Neal; pilot, CAA inspector and crop-dusting company owner George Eicher; and Victor Grisanti, pilot.

Crop-dusting planes were major users of the airport during the farming season, and Delta often had several dusters here.

In April 1942, Mayor Tom J. Harris was the guest of Lieutenant Colonel John D. Frederick, the camp commander, as five companies of army soldiers from Camp Redland (the current Homestead Housing Authority property) paraded on Homestead's municipal airport. The army had moved the unit to Homestead to protect U.S. 1 from Homestead to Key West and its bridges from saboteurs and to provide security at the new Homestead Army Air Field under construction.

After the war, in March 1946, the Homestead Airport Committee was composed of W.R. Bird, Lonnie Hood and Russell Horne, and on April 3, 1946, two former World War II WASPs (Women Airforce Service Pilots) made local history. They lifted their Norseman plane from Homestead's Municipal Airport and landed eleven hours later at LaGuardia Field in New York with 1,500 pounds of plants from the Paul F. Oskierko Nursery on Hainlin Mill Drive.

In August 1946, a plan was to be worked out for development of the municipal airport. W.O. Van Tien, owner and operator of a flying school, applied for a permit to build a twenty-plane hangar with service and maintenance facilities, and Meeks' Flying Service asked to expand its facilities. In September, Tien, also owner and operator of the South Dade Flying Service, and George Eicher of the Hall Dusting Company applied to fill the airport manager's job without pay. George was selected to manage the airport. The Homestead Municipal Airport was officially closed in 1952, but some use continued for a time, as evidenced by photos taken by Marlow Jacobsen.

MAYOR TOM HARRIS

A history of Homestead would not be complete without special note of longtime mayor Thomas J. Harris, or Mayor Tom, as he was affectionately called. One of the premier parks in Miami-Dade County is Harris Field at U.S. 1 and Southwest Eighth Street (Campbell Drive).

Born in Houston, Texas, Harris came to Homestead in 1915 as a young man and worked in the vegetable produce business. For part of his job, he would travel to Georgia to buy peaches, and rather than stay in hotels, he roomed with families as he moved around the state. On one trip, he took a room with the Bush family, and in 1921, he married their beautiful daughter Rosa Nell. Just days after the 1926 hurricane, Tom and Rosa were blessed with Thomas J. Harris Jr., their only child. They later built a fine home on Kings Highway that still stands today. She was his partner in all he did.

In 1936, after ten years of managing the packinghouse of Hardee & Gentile, Tom became a partner in the Hardee & Harris packinghouse. Captain Hardee was the predominant tomato grower on the East Coast, and the packinghouse was one of the largest of its time. From at least 1939 until 1944, Tom was chairman of the board of directors of the First National Bank of Homestead.

Mayor Tom served as mayor from 1937 until 1948 and then again from 1956 until 1961. He was a man with an ability to anticipate unforeseen outcomes in proposed city actions. Community leader J.T. Godwin remembered him as a wonderful, compassionate man, a straight shooter who was very knowledgeable of city finances.

In his last year as mayor, on August 21, 1961, Harris posed with Mae West who was in town celebrating the opening of the Krome Avenue Extension north of the Tamiami Trail. Florida governor Bryant dedicated the extension with her help. For many attendees, her star status upstaged the Seminole Indians and the U.S. Air Force personnel who were also part of the ceremony. Tongue-in-cheek, Mae West attributed her youthful figure to bike riding. Homestead was promoting itself as the "City of Bicycles," and you can ask Ruth Campbell. She was there and also posed for a photo with Mae West.

James Archer Smith Hospital

The first mention of what became James Archer Smith Hospital was in July 1938 when the *Homestead Leader Enterprise* reported that the city was planning a hospital as a WPA project. Local man Clarence J. Parman was the architect, and County Commissioner J.D. Redd donated the land. By November of that year, the WPA and FDR had approved a $46,000 hospital.

The ten-bed James Archer Smith Hospital opened August 9, 1940, on Northwest First Avenue, and Redland pioneer resident William Brodie was the first patient. Drs. Smith, Tower and A.M. Logan staffed it. One-third of the original cost was paid by the federal government and two-thirds by the community using private solicitations and holding fundraising fish fries and

The original James Archer Smith Hospital (a WPA project) opened August 9, 1940. The ten-room hospital was designed pro bono by Homestead architect Clarence J. Parman.

dinners. The *Leader Enterprise* reported: "Dr. Smith, for whom the hospital was named, and through whose efforts in raising money and stimulating public interest, it became a reality, said that the operating room, delivery room and service units are equipped on par with the best hospitals of the state. All the equipment is modern and was obtained without regard to price." Dr. Smith and Preston B. Bird "fathered" the hospital idea more than a year before it became a reality, and it was operated as a nonprofit organization with a volunteer board of directors. In 1944, a new wing added nine beds and a new kitchen.

In 1948, the JASH Auxiliary was formed by the Soroptomist Club of Homestead, headed by Mrs. Ben Archer; Mrs. B.A. Tibbitts became the first auxiliary president. Over the years, the auxiliary contributed significantly to the needs of the hospital and its patients. Dr. C.F. Robinson, a retired medical doctor, was the chairman of the hospital board, and Mrs. Rachael Wells was the hospital superintendent in 1949.

In 1949, the bed capacity increased to twenty-five by converting private rooms into semi-private rooms. In 1951, another wing provided thirty additional beds through the generosity and voluntary labor provided by the community. The auxiliary established a gift shop in 1961 under the direction of Miss Bertha N. Hausman and Charlotte (Mrs. Richard) Schmunk with many of the proceeds contributed to the hospital.

In 1967, there were plans to replace the original JASH with a 75-bed hospital through ownership by the City of Homestead. The three-story replacement building, using Federal Hill–Burton funds, was completed in March 1969. A new wing added in 1974 increased the bed capacity to 120. Hospital board members were: Orville Haller, chairman; Yvonne Brassfield; Paul Brookshire; Bea Peskoe; Reverend J. Elwood Rawls; George Skall; Dr. J.A. Smith; and Dr. Danilo Magtira. John Allinson was the administrator.

THE 1935 HURRICANE

In the midst of struggles, the September 2, 1935 hurricane that devastated the Florida Keys did mostly wind damage to fruit trees, telephone and electric wires in the Homestead area. Homestead was greatly involved in the aftermath, however.

According to the *Leader Enterprise* of September 6, the first organized rescue efforts were accomplished by Homestead area men on September 3. Between the early evening hours of Tuesday and early morning hours of the following day, 105 injured persons were transported from south of Snake Creek to Plantation Key by David Barnes using his outboard motorboat. Homestead's Dr. James Archer Smith was the first medical doctor on the scene.

Mayor Preston "Bunny" Bird organized the Homestead rescue party, which included: J.L. Scarborough, Foy Hobbs, R.E. Sherard, Fletcher Bryant, Ovid Sullivan, "Timmy" Hearndon, Thomas "Pink" Lamb, Buck Vaughan, Rolland McGregor, John Doughit, Jimmy Laster, James Simmons, Deacon Green, J.D. Redd, Archer Smith and Charles Caves. The evacuees were processed through the Sunday school rooms of the First Baptist Church of Homestead, now occupied by ArtSouth.

Myrtle Hodge, age fifteen, and her sister Sarah, thirteen, the daughters of Homestead's Mr. and Mrs. G.M. Hodge, were visiting in the Keys when the hurricane hit. It was not until late November that Myrtle's body was found on Bony Key, thirty-two miles northwest of Islamorada. A memorial service for the Hodge sisters was conducted by First Baptist pastor C.N. Walker, assisted by Homestead school principal L.B. Sommers.

Local pastors A.A. Koestline of the Homestead Methodist Church, Alfred McDonald of Sacred Heart Catholic Church and Rabbi Kaplan of Miami conducted services at each of three funeral pyres before the pyres were set afire. A Florida National Guard firing squad fired a rifle salute over the pyres of stacked-up "pine boxes containing the remains of civilians and veterans,

Protestants and Catholics, Gentile and Jew." The hurricane victims were cremated in mass to avoid the spread of disease.

Homestead officials took advantage of the hurricane to replace their 1917 American LaFrance fire truck, which was destroyed in a fire in April 1935. There was a nearly new 1933 Seagraves fire truck owned by the federal government at the Veterans Rehabilitation Camp on Matecumbe Key. After the hurricane, the slightly damaged truck was found at the Matecumbe Hotel.

Homestead city officials pushed the truck to the Islamorada Post Office, where it remained in the charge of nineteen-year old local boy Glenn Simmons, who guarded it for two weeks at two dollars per day. When city officials failed to return for it, Glenn left the truck unguarded and angry officials then returned for it. Glenn did not remember how it was transported to Homestead.

Negotiations to acquire the fire truck took place between Homestead city officials and the district head of the Federal Emergency Relief Administration, for whom the fire truck was originally ordered. In early December, Homestead received permission to keep the truck, which served Homestead well until the city turned its fire department over to Dade County. Eventually Jack Levy and the Homestead Lions Club acquired the truck and painted it Lions Club purple. It ended its life at Jack's Redland home.

PEARL HARBOR, DECEMBER 7, 1941

In looking back to the actual entry of the United States into World War II, the attack by the Japanese on Pearl Harbor and other Pacific Ocean targets shocked our nation, but people in Homestead were already seeing war preparation actions being taken.

Local young men and women had been enlisting in the armed forces in large numbers. Many were being selected for the aviation field, others were drafted and college students were offered free flying training. President Franklin Delano Roosevelt and his senior advisors saw our weakness in the field of military aviation when compared with Nazi Germany and Japan. In the late 1930s, there were fewer than twenty military airfields and over seven hundred at the end of World War II.

The land at Pine Island east of Homestead being cleared for a civil airfield had a military use in mind, and the 135-mile freshwater pipeline from southwest of Florida City to Key West was to provide fresh water for the boilers of navy ships.

Politically, Homestead was at its apex. Local men chaired the Dade County Commission and the Dade County School Board in the persons of J.D. Redd, who had already served eighteen years on the commission and as its chair once before, and C.G. Turner on the school board. Additionally, Homestead Councilman F.B. Rue served on the county's important Budget Board.

Growth in Homestead's population was at 36 percent between 1930 and 1940, and Florida City's was at 66 percent. Although Homestead's population on December 7, 1941, was only between 3,100 and 3,500, the Japanese attack profoundly impacted six Homestead area families.

At Pearl Harbor, Anderson Arrant and Earl Smith were serving in USS *Arizona*, James Field was serving in USS *Indianapolis*, Walter Thompson Jr. was a marine and Lieutenant John M. Lee was assigned to the cruiser USS *Boise*. It was five weeks before the Arrant and Smith families knew for certain of their sons' deaths. At that time, a memorial service was held at the First Baptist Church of Homestead.

Louis Biondo, who was serving in the army in the Philippines, was captured by the Japanese, survived the brutal Bataan Death March and was a prisoner of war for the duration of World War II.

By October 1943, 59 men and women from Homestead High School faculty had joined the navy, including Ted Bleier, C.H. Rice, Josephine Cook and two women who became WAVES: Birdie Horne and Bessie Chambliss. This from a small city of 3,500 people at most!

Anderson Arrant and Earl Smith were both awarded the Purple Heart posthumously in 1944, but it was not until 1948 that Earl Smith's remains were returned to the United States. Anderson Arrant's remains are probably entombed in USS *Arizona* with hundreds of his shipmates. In 1945, the new Veterans of Foreign Wars Post 4127 was named the Arrant-Smith VFW Post 4127.

Louis Biondo was liberated from a Japanese POW camp in 1945 and returned home. Also liberated in 1945 at the same time was Navy Machinist Mate First Class Donald Smith. Nothing further is available in local records about Donald Smith.

FAMOUS ENTERTAINERS STOP IN HOMESTEAD

Al Jolson was one of the greatest entertainers of his time, known as "the Jazz Singer," and Ben Bernie was a violinist and big band leader of the Ben Bernie Orchestra. In yet another one of history's interesting side notes, Jolson and Bernie registered for the draft in Homestead on April 27, 1942, at Neva King Cooper School on the way to Key West to perform for the USO. Why? Because on a certain date, men were required to register for the draft, no matter where they were.

HOMESTEAD DURING WORLD WAR II

During World War II, the major change to Homestead and South Dade was the construction of Homestead Army Air Field and the navy's fresh water pipeline. Local people were also involved in the construction of the Naval Air Station at Richmond and as employees of that base. At its peak, the population of the Homestead Army Air Field was just over three thousand, matching its host city.

In all, over six hundred Redland District men and women served in uniform in World War II. The twenty-two who gave their lives were: Ray Andrews, Anderson Arrant, Benjamin F. Bechtol, Kenneth Chambers, R.H. Donovan, Charles E. Eichenberger Jr., Gerald Lane, Clayton E. Lehman, Ballard Lewis, John W. Little, James L. Loper, Hardee R. Mills, Tommy Moffett, Marlin Moore, Joseph L. Piche, Edward Schultz, Charles Sellers, Rupert Shelly, Earl W. Smith, Earl Swilley, Jefferson F. Thomas and Norris A. Walker.

In fact, in recognition of the heroic life of Ensign Charles Emil Eichenberger, who was killed in action September 12, 1942, in the Pacific, the U.S. Navy named a destroyer escort after him. The USS *Eichenberger*, DE 202, fittingly took the fight to the Japanese in Southeast Asia and around the Philippine Islands. His widow christened the ship on November 17, 1943, at the Charleston Navy Yard. The *Eichenberger*, lovingly called the "Fightin' Eich" by its crew made up of 15 officers and 158 enlisted, earned four battle stars as it provided valuable escort protection to carrier task groups and to other ships. After the war, it was put into mothballs and sold for scrap in 1973.

Although not in uniform, many local people, particularly women, were employed at the base, thus freeing up military men to serve in war zones.

In 1943, a WAC company of about forty to fifty women had perhaps even greater impact, freeing up men from jobs in transportation, administration and air traffic control for overseas assignments.

Homestead was a welcoming host to HAAF personnel. Wives and children of men assigned to the base often moved to Homestead for the short periods of time the men trained here before overseas assignments. With every available space (including garages and attics) rented, some of the officers lived in Coral Gables and Miami.

Local groups entertained the troops at the base and those guarding the bridges to the Keys. The Junior Woman's Club of Homestead led the way to form a USO unit in the chamber of commerce's Fruit Festival building. They and others in the community donated furniture, pianos, lamps, books, radios and other items to outfit day rooms in the barracks at HAAF for recreation. Bus service between the base and Homestead was set up, and buses running from Miami to Homestead added a stop at the base.

Homestead did what most cities of its size did to support the war effort. First National Bank of Homestead's Max Losner led war bond drives that regularly outperformed other communities. The army air force from HAAF and the navy from Naval Air Station Richmond led war bond parades with Scouts and the Homestead High School marching band. Drives for scrap metal and rubber were enthusiastically supported by Boy and Girl Scout troops, high schools, the Rotary and Lions Clubs and churches. Homestead High won a $100 prize for collecting 211,313 pounds of scrap, and Redland High collected 167,737 pounds in a 1942 drive. Those are astronomic numbers!

Air raid wardens worked closely with those living in their districts. Eight wooden air observation towers from Perrine south were manned twenty-four hours a day, seven days a week by civilian volunteers—men, women and children. One of the most proficient spotters with regard to aircraft identification was eleven-year-old Kenny Graves. Reverend M.E. Myer, pastor of Silver Palm United Methodist Church, supervised the seventeen volunteers of the Redland tower. Miss LaNelle Rogers, the reigning Miss Redland, won second place in the "Sweetheart of the Air Corps for 1942" competition at the Blackstone Hotel in Miami Beach.

The Dade County Defense Council set up and supplied an emergency surgical station at Homestead City Hall with volunteer doctors: A.M. Logan, Frank Hausman, R.J. Elliott and C.H. Denby. Nurses were Mrs. James L. Nesbitt, Mrs. M.E. Stevens, Mrs. J.R. Brooks, Mrs. G.O. Brewster, Mrs. A.M. Logan, Mrs. W.A. Kopp and Mrs. B.A. Tibbets. Dr. James Archer Smith was probably not included since he had higher duties as Dade County physician and surgeon. The Fuchs Baking Company made its thirty-six bakery trucks available for emergency ambulances.

A home guard unit was formed in Redland to perform National Guard–like defense functions, and the American Red Cross unit in Homestead was busy throughout the war supporting our men and women in uniform. Local men and women served as volunteer members of Draft and Rationing Boards, not always popular duties.

The return of our veterans from World War II signaled a new period of vitality and strength in our great city of Homestead.

VETERANS OF FOREIGN WARS POST ESTABLISHED

Veterans returning from World War II established Homestead's first VFW post in 1945 and constructed a building at 601 Northeast Second Road on land donated by the City of Homestead. James C. Vann was the first VFW commander. Post 4127 was named for young Homestead men Anderson Arrant and Earl Smith, who were both killed in USS *Arizona* during the Japanese attack on Pearl Harbor. The post sponsored the first Armistice Day (now Veterans' Day) parade in 1946.

MORE ABOUT THE BASE

The importance of aviation in Homestead deserves a detailed look. Navy, marine and army aviation first came to the Miami area around World War I because of the training opportunities made possible by our excellent flying weather.

By comparison with Germany's expansion of the Luftwaffe in the 1930s, the programs of the European countries were both modest and slow. These countries had excellent new types under development, but too few aircraft had come off our lines before the outbreak of war. The British Purchasing Mission in 1938 ordered great numbers of American aircraft. Most of us are familiar with the fifty destroyers sent to the United Kingdom under the Lend-Lease Act, which Congress approved in March 1941, but it also permitted the donation of aircraft to the Allies.

South Dade County Airport became Homestead Army Airfield in 1942. The airfield served with distinction during World War II but was destroyed by the 1945 hurricane.

Homestead Army Airfield Control Towers and Hangars #1, 2 and 3. The tracked vehicles (left) were used to rescue airmen when they went down over land.

Troops from Homestead Army Airfield on Krome Avenue during a war bond parade.
Courtesy Captain Tom Royal Collection, thanks to the Rotary Club.

Before the entry of the United States into World War II, Pan American
Air Ferries, Inc., a subsidiary of Pan American Airlines, pioneered the
ferrying of aircraft abroad to our allies under an army contract. Almost
all the transport and many bomber aircraft used by the Allied powers were
produced by U.S. industry.

As mentioned earlier, South Dade County Airport east of Homestead
was constructed using Civil Air Authority funding. Despite an isolationist
congress, President Roosevelt was able to construct a large number of
airports, which were projected to be for military use should the need
arise. Homestead's airport was one of those because city fathers took the
initiative to create an airfield. In fact, Preston B. "Bunny" Bird, a very
visionary community leader, can really be called the father of the base
since he brought the idea of creating the airfield to the Homestead City
Council in May 1940.

When the airfield was taken over in September 1942 by the Army Air
Corps and named Homestead Army Air Field, its initial complement of 4
officers and 8 enlisted increased to 64 officers and 880 enlisted by November
1942. Concurrently, the Pan American civilian employees were militarized

and considerable construction was begun. In November, the first aircraft, thirty-three Douglas A20 medium bombers, were sent overseas.

To provide for a surge in personnel, the adjacent South Dade Migratory Farm Labor Camp, which had just been constructed for black farmworkers, was leased from the Farm Security Administration and converted into the "Ground School area."

Homestead Army Air Field trained Air Transport Command air crews, served as a jumping-off point for the shuttling of aircraft to the European allies and was a major U.S. terminus for the transport of critical materiel to Europe, the Middle East and China. Toward the end of the war, it was a training base for the Air Transport Command, the predecessor of Military Airlift Command. In August 1944, at its World War II peak, 340 officers and 2,617 enlisted men and women were stationed at the base, and HAAF was called the "West Point of Air Transport Command."

In May 1944, C46 Commandos arrived for use in two-engine aircraft training but were then replaced with four-engine C54 Skymasters, some B24 Liberators and C87 Liberator transports (276 B24Ds were completed as C87 transports.) Beginning in 1945, combat pilots were returned to Homestead from overseas to transition to transport aircraft. These pilots were to be trained to fly from short airstrips on small islands or in jungles. Satellite fields on Vaca Key (Marathon) and Immokalee were used to simulate these conditions.

Chapter 4

THE CHANGING FACE OF HOMESTEAD

A hurricane in mid-September of 1945 actually set the stage for the closure of Homestead Army Air Field post–World War II. All flyable aircraft were sent to other bases and most of the men and women evacuated. Those who remained set up a command post in a hurricane-proof building against winds reaching 140 miles per hour. Massive destruction caused HAAF to be formally closed on December 14, 1945, and returned to Dade

Landon Carney's Packing House on North Flagler, just north of Tucci's Packing House was among buildings damaged during the 1945 hurricane. *Courtesy A.F. Webb Family Collection.*

County after World War II. For several years, weather slowly destroyed the buildings and the field became overgrown as unattended land does here. To quote an air force history: "Like the abandoned site of a gold rush after the last vein has petered out, it lay deserted and reclaimed by nature."

Despite efforts by Homestead community leaders to make the base reuse a success, they appeared to be fighting a losing battle. Time, however, did prove to be on their side in this case.

THE STRATEGIC AIR COMMAND ERA

The new Strategic Air Command (SAC) came and surveyed the base in 1953 for possible use, reestablished it in June 1953 and formally dedicated it in 1956. SAC chose Homestead because of its South Florida location, semi-tropical weather and rehabilitation costs that were 11 percent below the national average. It acquired 1,200 acres of land in 1954, doubling the base size, and the first SAC unit, the Air Base Squadron, was activated here in 1955. Of 197 buildings on base, 96 were torn down and 51 scheduled for rehabilitation. Base acreage increased from 2,400 to 3,800 in 1959.

The official air show and ceremony reopening Homestead Air Force Base on June 23, 1956, featured the finest Strategic Air Command aircraft (B-47 front, B-36 rear).

HOMESTEAD AFB IS A PERMANENT INSTALLATION! ran the December 2, 1954 headline. The base was to be a permanent two-wing, medium bomber base, projected to be fully operational in 1956 with troop strength expected to increase beginning in the summer of 1955. Base Commander Colonel Robert S. Kittel felt both the base and local economies would benefit, as additional housing would have to be built. A survey of private builders' housing was taken so it could be determined how much government-financed housing was needed under the Wherry Act. (Housing by the West Gate was built as a result of this new designation and upgraded mission.) Colonel Kittel estimated that at least 2,000 rental units would be needed, and the air force had only 700 units in a request before Congress. The first families began moving into the Wherry Housing by the West Gate in the fall of 1958. Over time, 1,600 units of housing were built and two nine-hole golf courses were added.

BASE REOPENED

Homestead Air Force Base was reopened officially on June 22, 1956, with a dedication ceremony and an air show featuring SAC's finest aircraft. Brigadier General Keith K. Compton, commanding general of Homestead's 823rd Division, introduced U.S. Senator Spessard Holland, U.S. Representative Dante Fascell, Major General Francis H. Griswold (vice commander of SAC) and Major General Frank A. Armstrong (second air force commander). An estimated forty thousand people toured various aircraft static displays, including a KC97 tanker, a B47 Stratojet and the giant B36 intercontinental bomber. Four F-84s passed over the crowd showing what they could do. Other air power demonstrations included B47s in refueling, a V formation of three B36s and a B47 in a maximum performance take-off. The only disappointment was that the USAF Thunderbirds did not arrive in time for the show.

B47 MEDIUM JET BOMBERS

Colonel Twitty, base commander, met with Homestead residents in January 1956 to dispel concern over the noise generated by the B47s. Residents were surprised to learn that B47s had already been active for about a week. Twitty said the northeast-southwest orientation of the runway and a right-hand traffic pattern diverted aircraft away from developed areas.

The 19th Air Refueling Squadron that flew the KC97, SAC's mobile gas station, in support of medium and heavy bomber units, was activated in February 1956 and tapped to become a part of the 379th Bombardment Wing with Lieutenant Colonel William E. Smith as the commander. Later models of the aircraft designed to carry troops, cargo and a hospital were scheduled to follow the KC97s. The 19th Bombardment Wing, located at Pinecastle Air Force Base near Orlando, was soon notified to relocate to Homestead by the end of June 1956. The outfit, with three squadrons, saw three years of action during the Korean Conflict.

By the end of the 1950s, the base had more than six thousand members, twice the size of its busiest World War II days, a fleet of ninety B47 Stratojets and a squadron of KC97 tankers.

There were several barracks, an administration building and a wooden hangar when construction began on the big hangar and maintenance shops. With no electricity to the runway, fifty-five-gallon oil drums were painted with international orange and spaced on both sides of the runway to assist the B47 crews in lining up. Now, two combat-ready bomb wings of Strategic Air Command, each consisting of forty-five B47 bombers, occupied the base. Their mission, named "Reflex," was to supplement the alert force in Africa and to train new crews. Each wing would dispatch two combat-ready aircraft each week on a rotation basis. A squadron of KC97s was also stationed on the base.

By June 1960, the 379th Bomb Wing was transferred to Wurtsmith Air Force Base in Michigan, and the B47 bombers were also reassigned to make way for the B52 Stratofortresses. During a brief shutdown of the base, the runway was extended to approximately twelve thousand feet and reinforced to accommodate the heavier bomber. The plane, often called the "BUFF," would be a familiar sight for the next eight years. [*Author's note:* Since this is a G-rated book, if you're curious about what "BUFF" stands for, ask anyone who has spent time around the B-52 bomber.]

Hurricanes like the September 1960 Hurricane Donna continued to impact HAFB operations. The remaining B47s began flying out at 0800, September 8 at five-minute intervals, and by 0430 on September 9, operations became very inactive. Donna blew winds up to seventy-three miles per hour and dumped 10.69 inches of rainfall, resulting in $500,000 of damage.

In early 1962, the first B52H arrived at Homestead AFB from the Boeing Aircraft Company with the governor of Florida aboard. Soon thereafter, the mayor of Homestead rode in on the first KC135 Stratotanker that would replace the KC97s.

The mission of Homestead AFB changed with the B52s. The Nineteenth Bomb Wing was assigned to fly the "Dew Line" of Northern Canada and Alaska, to react to any threat by Russia. This necessitated the construction of the Alert Crew Ready Building. Crews were assigned alert status of seven days, and the bombers were to be airborne within fifteen minutes. Two combat-ready B52H bomber aircraft launched every day at 1500 hours to fly a twenty-four-hour mission without landing, supported by air refueling aircraft. They landed at 1530 hours each day after their replacement departed.

In March 1962, the Thirty-first Tactical Fighter Wing moved with its F-100 Supersabres from California to Homestead in response to the growing communist threat from Cuba. The Air Defense Command also sent in F102 Delta Daggers, which stayed through the Cuban Crisis of the fall of 1962 until March 1963 when they were replaced by F104 Starfighters. In April 1962, Hound Dog, the first guided aircraft missile had arrived.

In February 1964, the Thirty-first TFW made air force history by flying F100s nonstop from Homestead to Turkey for the longest mass flight of jet aircraft across the Atlantic. The 6,600-mile flight took eleven and a half hours and eight in-flight refuelings. In late 1966, the Thirty-first transferred to Tuy Hoa Air Base—235 miles northeast of Saigon on the South China Sea—where it served with distinction. The wing returned to Homestead in late 1970 and shifted to F4Es.

When Strategic Air Command was reorganized in 1968, the aircraft were dispersed to scattered locations, including many air force bases and some civilian airports. This was required to protect the grouping of these aircraft.

On July 1, 1968, Tactical Air Command assumed control of the base, and the Thirty-first Tactical Fighter Wing became the host unit, as the base continued to grow and expand its role as a tactical fighter wing. The AF Reserve units, Air National Guard, U.S. Naval Security Group Activity and the AF Command Conference Center were established on base. In March 1981, the mission role was changed to one of a training wing, utilizing the F-4D Phantom II jet fighter. In October 1985, the Thirty-first regained its role as a "fighter" wing with the F-16 mission. With two combat-ready fighter squadrons, Homestead AFB stood ready to project tactical air power whenever and wherever it was called upon to do so.

Air Reserve Airborne Early Warning

The Seventy-ninth Military Airlift Squadron was redesignated the Seventy-ninth Airborne Early Warning and Control Squadron (AEW&CS) on July 30, 1971, and had its C124 cargo planes replaced with EC121Ds. The EC121D, with radomes above and below the aircraft fuselage and six tons of electronic surveillance equipment, was a modified military version of Lockheed's Constellation commercial plane. The Seventy-ninth's mission was to provide "airborne radar surveillance and tactical control of air defense weapons for air defense and contingency operations." Initially, the squadron air crews flew missions in the Caribbean and Gulf of Mexico. In 1974, the Seventy-ninth converted to EC121Ts and sent its "D" models to the Military Aircraft Storage and Disposition Center at Davis Monthan Air Force Base in Arizona.

In 1976, the Reserve early warning program underwent significant changes. Although the air force wished to terminate its EC121 Iceland mission for economy purposes, the Office of the Secretary of Defense requested that the air force continue the mission pending other arrangements. Accordingly, the air force assigned the Seventy-ninth responsibility for flying missions out of Keflavik, Iceland, on a rotational basis.

The Aerospace Defense Command activated Detachment 1 of the 20th Air Defense Squadron on March 1, 1976, to support the Reserve effort. This augmentation by active-duty air crews and support personnel in effect became an active associate program, the reverse of the Reserve associate program begun in 1968. Associate units do not own their own aircraft; instead unit personnel fly and maintain those belonging to co-located units. On December 1, 1976, the Reserve activated the 915th Airborne Group (AEW&CG) at Homestead Air Force Base to provide control and command supervision over the 79th AEW&CS.

In 1978, the air force ended the EC121 Iceland and Florida missions once E-3A AWACS aircraft entered the aircraft inventory, and the Air Force Reserve began converting its EC121 units to fighter operations.

Effective October 1, 1978, Headquarters Air Force Reserve redesignated the 915th AEW&CG as a tactical fighter group and inactivated the 79th AEW&CS, replacing it at Homestead AFB with the 93rd Tactical Fighter Squadron, the Reserve's first F-4C equipped unit.

Hurricane Andrew Changed Everything

After Hurricane Andrew destroyed the base in August 1992, the next serious threat came from the Base Realignment and Closure Committee (BRACC), which sought to close the ravaged base. The civilian community mustered its support of the base and launched a fight for the base's very survival and the return of the fighter operations to South Florida. The BRACC withdrew Homestead Air Force Base from the closure list.

The Air Force Ball held on March 5, 1994, was a bittersweet event. The event was a "Hail and Farewell" to "hail" the return of the 482nd fighter wing from its post-Andrew exile to MacDill Air Force Base, Florida, to its new role as the predominant unit at the "new" Homestead Air Reserve Base and to bid "farewell" to the 31st TFW. The 31st TFW was deactivated at Homestead AFB and reactivated at Aviano Airbase in Italy.

Homestead AFB was re-designated as Homestead ARB on March 31, 1994. The base serves many critical Homeland Security purposes and is home to several units with like missions, including two active duty units.

Retracing Steps to Non-Military Events

As important as the base was, many other major events followed the end of World War II. The Everglades National Park was established June 20, 1947, in Washington, D.C., when Secretary of the Interior J.A. King signed the papers. On December 5, 1947, the stamp commemorating the establishment of Everglades National Park was issued. The post office was located in the old Edward Stiling Real Estate Office on the corner of Palm Drive and Third Avenue, and Florida City postmistress Mrs. Anna B. Chapman is said to have handled over one million pieces of mail. There were so many first-day covers mailed they were put into field crates. Of more than fifty different Everglades FDC designs known to exist, many have been collected by the Florida Pioneer Museum.

From the program at Florida City for the First Day of Issue 3-cent stamp honoring the occasion:

> *The ceremony took place at 9:30AM in front of the City Hall. Dan L. Meeker, President of the Redland District Chamber of Commerce was the master of ceremonies and the Homestead High School Band performed.*

*Rev. Father Paul Manning of Sacred Heart Church gave the invocation
and Rev. Robert B. Chapman, Jr. of Florida City Community Church
gave the benediction. Mayor Herbert Hunter of Florida gave the welcome.
Thomas J. Allen, Regional Director, National Park Service gave remarks
as did Florida Governor Millard F. Caldwell. Miami Florida Postmaster
High P. Emerson introduced the Postmaster General Robert E. Hannegan
who gave the address. Stamp albums were presented by the Third Assistant
Postmaster Joseph J. Lawler to Governor Millard Caldwell, Senator
Claude Pepper, Senator Spessard L. Holland and Mr. Paul R. Scott, Mr.
Will N. Preston, and Mr. John D. Pennekamp. The Response was given
by Paul R. Scott.*

As a part of formalizing the Everglades National Park, the first
headquarters were set up by the first superintendent, Dan Beard Jr., in the
Redland District Chamber of Commerce Fruit Festival Building.

ESTABLISHING THE COUNTRY'S SOUTHERNMOST RODEO

The first rodeo in Homestead was sponsored by the Elks Lodge under the
direction of Dr. R.J. Elliott and held at the Municipal Park. The Elks turned
over the $1,000 profit to Jack Bell of the *Miami Herald* for use by Variety
Children's Hospital in November 1949.

There was no rodeo in 1950, and the Homestead Jaycees, under the
direction of John McLean, Bob Morgan and Dr. R.J. Elliott, sponsored the
second rodeo on Saturday, February 10, 1951, at 8:00 p.m. and Sunday,
February 11, 1951, at 2:30 p.m. Jim Sharp was listed as president of the rodeo
and Vernon Turner as secretary/treasurer. Attendance was eight thousand,
a disappointment because of bad weather, although three thousand children
attended "Kids Day" (probably Saturday afternoon). A street dance on
Friday night kicked off festivities. The rodeo queen was Georgia Skall, and
Buck and his trained bear performed as entertainment, although a Brahma
bull broke loose and did extensive damage. Despite the seemingly good gate,
receipts did not cover expenses.

In January 1952, Jaycees president Ralph Matousek announced there were
insufficient financial resources to have a rodeo. On February 1, the Homestead
Rodeo Association as we know it today was formed by seventeen men:

Jim Sharp
Al Webber
Dr. R.J. Elliott
Al Goding
Pat Rutherford
Joe Perkins
Bill Mitchell
Dr. John DeMilly
William Sottile
Ken Doherty
Whitney Beam
Tom Hodson
Everett Douberly
Vernon Turner
George Skall
John Hale
Earl Gordon Sr.

The Homestead Rodeo Association presented its first rodeo on March 8 and 9, 1952, and according to their records, it was with Jim Sharp and Dr. R.J. Elliott in charge and "Runt Smith, a Homestead boy, as rodeo director." Association members Elliott, Sharp, Webber and Beam and their wives went to look over the Davie rodeo and get ideas. The HRA's first successful rodeo was endorsed by the Redland District Chamber of Commerce, and E. Pardee, who reportedly "provided shows and stock for Gene Autrey," provided the stock for the rodeo. Records show that the Homestead Posse, with thirty members, was organized as an outgrowth of the Redland Riding Club, which was started in 1950 by Dr. R.J. Elliott. "Posse Top Hands" were: Whitney Beam, Al Webber, Jim Sharp, Mr. Dolar, Mr. Sharp (not Jim), E. Carter, Earl Gordon, "Runt" Smith, Mr. Carter (probably Bob Carter), Mr. Feeny and Mr. Danzey.

On August 15, 1952, George Skall made the proposal for the HRA asking the city for a rodeo site, but officials objected to using the ballpark for rodeos and circuses. The next month, Jim Sharp (listed as HRA president), announced the lease of a five-acre tract just southeast of the ballpark from South Dade Farms. The second rodeo of 1952 was already planned for November 8, 1952, but October rains forced postponement until November 29.

The new arena was outfitted with $11,000 in new bleachers and other improvements. Dr. R.J. Elliott became HRA president with Bill Mitchell as

Arcade Cafeteria was located in the 401 Building at Krome Avenue and Fourth Street.
Arcade Cafeteria opened on December 29, 1956, and was later called Barnett's Cafeteria.

vice-president and Bill Sottile as secretary/treasurer. The posse's youngest performer was Steve Beam, and other riders included the Sharps, the Webbers, Bob Carter and Roger and Ken Glenn. However, with an attendance of 6,500 and expenses slightly exceeding income, rodeo members struggled to pay the $11,000 debt. Happily, HRA funding later improved.

In other post–World War II economic matters, South Dade Farmers Bank opened in its new building on South Krome Avenue on October 12, 1951, a building constructed by South Dade Farms (owned by James Sottile Sr.). Luther Chandler was its president; Robert A. Freitag, executive vice-president; Walter E. Loper, cashier; Edward J. Van Houten, assistant cashier; Thelma Turner McGarrah, secretary; Aida Liken, bookkeeper-accountant; and Kay Peterson and Mildred Legett, tellers. The founding directors were Preston B. Bird, George H. Cooper, Alonzo Cothron, W.J. Fowler, M. Lewis Hall, L.I. Hood, Adrian Jacobs, William Sottile and Vernon Turner.

In October 1960, the bank was purchased by a group of South Dade businessmen headed by the bank's board of directors. The new directors were James Sottile Sr., board chairman; Mason Alger; J. Rudolph Gossman; William Sottile; J.H. Cornelius; Barney Howard; Vernon W. Turner; Jefferson Davis; and Joseph S. Moss. It later became the Bank of Florida and then Barnett Bank. The officers were Barney Howard, president; Douglas McAllister, vice-president; Thelma Turner Suttard, assistant vice-president; Cecelia Harper, cashier; and Myerrah Freh and Grace Johnson, assistant cashiers.

The Sottiles owned seven more South Florida banks: Pan American, Bank of Miami, Coral Gables First National, American National Bank of Fort Lauderdale, Boynton Beach State Bank, Bank of Palmetto and Avon Park Citrus Bank. As a major landholder, approximately one-half of Sotille's 20,000 acres of tillable land east of Homestead was rented for cultivation. He ultimately donated 1,200 acres for Homestead Bayfront Park, 20 acres for the Florida City State Farmers' Market and 80 acres to the federal Farm Security Administration for construction of South Dade Labor Camp on East Campbell Drive.

POLICE CHIEF BRANTLEY KILLED

Homestead Police Chief William F. Brantley was killed in the line of duty March 16, 1952, when Douglas D. Carroll, a foreman at the state prison camp southwest of Florida City, opened fire on him at the Sullivan Nursery. Chief Brantley, a veteran of World War II, the Fort Meyers Police Force and the Florida Highway Patrol, became chief of the four-man police force in 1946. He was the second Homestead police chief killed in the line of duty.

ANOTHER NEW, BIGGER SCHOOL

On a less tragic note, in October 1951, drawings of the proposed "A.L. Lewis Elementary School for Negroes" were presented to the community. The new school, designed by architect William D. Bordeaux of Miami, was to consist of an administration department, library, cafetorium and fifteen classrooms. The exterior walls were to be of masonry, but the structure was to be framed with glued laminated wood, prefabricated at the factory, which was to affect a savings of erection time, thus reducing the over-all cost. Old, poorly maintained wooden buildings were replaced. Its namesake, A.L. Lewis, was a black millionaire insurance company owner. PTA officer the late Jessie Robinson Sr. stated that efforts to involve A.L. Lewis in the school failed. The school was later renamed the Laura C. Saunders Elementary School after a longtime principal.

MEXICAN AMERICAN FAMILIES ARRIVE

Until the arrival of the Mexican Americans in the 1950s, most of the farmworkers were blacks or Anglos from the southeastern states. During World War II and at other times, the farmers were successful in lobbying for the temporary entry of Bahamians to work on the farms and in the groves.

The Cosme Perez family is believed to be the first Mexican American family to arrive in South Dade around 1951. There are no written records, so oral histories have provided some information whose detail cannot be verified.

Among the families arriving in the mid-1950s were those of Jose Avalos, Burny Espinoza, Felipe Martinez, Margarito Martinez and Casimiro Valdez. The Cleo Deleon family arrived in December 1954. Others were Nestor Rodriguez, Isidro Saldiear and Felix Angurano. Many second-generation family members became elected officials, educators and successful business owners.

FIRST BLACK CANDIDATES FOR PUBLIC OFFICE

As a part of the early movement away from the traditional separation of the black and white communities, the first black man to file to run for election for the Homestead City Council was Henry Duhart, the owner of the Red Dot Café, 251 Southwest Fifth Street in Homestead. Born on a farm in Georgia, Duhart first came to Miami where he worked for the city sanitary department for nine years and at other times sold ice cream and worked as a laborer. He came to Homestead in 1945 with his wife and two children, one of school age. He was fifty-five years old when he decided to run for office in the 1955 election. The *Homestead News* reported that he was sponsored by the Negro Civic League, composed of some twenty-five to thirty members, with Romays Smith its president.

When asked by the *News* why he wanted to run for the council seat, Duhart said, "The Negro section has had no representation and that [I] would try to make the colored section a better place in which to live." Further, he pointed out that there were many bad streets in the section and inadequate lighting facilities. Just as candidates today do, he had been attending city council meetings as a spectator to get a line on the way business was handled by the city's administrators.

His plans were for an intensive drive to get all qualified voters in the black community to register and to "single shot" their votes, which meant that they would vote for only their one candidate—Henry Duhart. Homestead did not have districts at that time. The black community was thought to use the single-shot vote to ensure its voices were heard up until residential area districts were established in 2002.

In early November the *Homestead News* reported that "Raphu Williams, a controversial figure who has established a hotel in the S.W. section of the city and whose name has been in the headlines recently" had filed to run for city council. He may have been controversial because he fought and won a strange parking violation citation using a well-known Miami civil rights attorney.

According to the *Homestead News*, "Williams is a man with better than average educations background, holding a Master's Degree from Boston University. He is affiliated with the Elks, Phi Sigma Fraternity, Dade County Teachers Association, and is a 32 degree Mason."

Reporting more accurately, the *Homestead Leader-Enterprise* said that Raphu Williams held a bachelor's degree from Tuskeegee Institute and a master's degree from Boston University and he had taken graduate courses at Florida A&M University, Fitchburg State Teachers College, Suffolk University School of Law and Harvard University.

Williams was first a teacher in Dade County Public Schools and then principal of A.L. Lewis School in Homestead from 1939 to 1942. Later interested in real estate, he was a trustee of a realty group operating the Hotel Caroline Williams in the southwest section of Homestead. With his wife, Charlotte, he operated the Caroline Hotel and Restaurant and the Williams Boarding House in Homestead. He owned and operated a large Miami-based ambulance service that catered to the black community.

Both black candidates lost in the primary election—perhaps because they split the single-shot votes or because voters were not familiar with the single-shot process.

Twenty-one years, later in December 1975, Yvonne Brassfield, born in 1936, became Homestead's first black councilwoman elected for a two-year term. Like Raphu Williams, she was an educator. She had to attend George Washington Carver High School in Miami, however, due to the rules of segregation. When she graduated at only age fifteen, she then set her sights on Fisk University in Nashville and later became a teacher at West Homestead Junior High School. She was also former mayor Roscoe Warren's seventh-grade English teacher. Her father, James Howard, a businessman who owned considerable property, was a prominent figure in the black community. She was also the first black person to serve on the James Archer Smith Hospital board of directors. She lost her bid for reelection in 1977 by a margin of only seven votes.

INTERESTING HISTORY TIDBITS

Setting aside politics, however, an interesting note throughout the town's history has been that celebrities like pianist Roger Williams visited Homestead. He had the biggest hit ever for a pianist with his 1955 recording of "Autumn Leaves." When Roger visited an aunt living in Homestead, he would stop by the USO and play for the military men and women. In 1958 during the term of Woman's Club of Homestead president Mary Alice Branam, the women leased the Dade County Auditorium in Miami and sponsored a concert by Roger to benefit their free Homestead Children's Dental Clinic that was staffed by club members. The Soroptimist and Rotary Clubs of Homestead also contributed regularly to the clinic.

Hank Cutshall, local radio station personality, bandleader and former marine, was another favorite performer that Edna Blackstone, the USO director, often persuaded to play. Many of the men and women in uniform away from home addressed Edna as "Mom" Blackstone. Edna was very protective of her troops, gave tirelessly and was even feisty.

Chapter 5

FASTBALLS AND MISSILES

M ajor league baseball came to Homestead, probably for the first time on the first Saturday of April 1961; and the city was soon calling itself, "Homestead, the Baseball City." The St. Louis Cardinals were attracted to Homestead as a site for their minor league teams by the Homestead Redland District Chamber of Commerce. Dick Conley was president of Dick Conley Chevrolet and president of the chamber, and Merl Young was the executive director. (Conley later became mayor of Homestead.) Both men were very effective promoters of "Homestead and Florida City: South Florida's famous twin cities."

Stan Musial, the great Cardinals outfielder/first baseman, and outfielder Roberto Clemente of the 1960 world champion Pittsburgh Pirates played in the game at Harris Field, which the home team Cardinals won 4–3. The Cardinals fielded such greats as pitchers Curt Simmons and Bob Gibson, catcher Tim McCarver, infielders Ken Boyer and Red Schoendienst and outfielders Curt Flood and Stan Musial. They won eighty and lost seventy-four games, finishing fifth in the league. The Pirates fielded greats, such as pitchers Bob Friend, Harvey Haddix, Vinegar Bend Mizell and Bobby Shantz; infielders Bill Mazeroski and Dick Schofield; and outfielders Donn Clendenon and Bill Virdon. After their 1960 world series win, the Pirates finished sixth in the league with a seventy-five win, seventy-nine loss record.

Cardinals farm teams that carried out spring training in Homestead included the Puerto Rican Marlins and teams from Portland, Oregon; Tulsa,

A Saint Louis Cardinals brochure served as the inspiration for a Homestead and Florida City billboard that greeted visitors and residents alike.

Oklahoma; Lancaster, Pennsylvania; Winnipeg, Canada; Billings, Montana; Keokuk, Iowa; and Jefferson City, Tennessee.

A billboard announced Homestead, Florida, as the "Winter Home of the St. Louis Minor League Clubs," and many scouts and representatives of sporting goods manufacturers spent time in Homestead. Factory representatives signed budding stars to contracts to endorse their companies' bats, shoes and other equipment before they became stars and demanded higher contracts. Bettye and Ivan Cason, who ran the premier South Dade sporting goods store, remembered well the economic impact of spring training.

The Homestead Redland District Chamber of Commerce published a full-color brochure touting not only Tom J. Harris Field as the winter home of the St. Louis Cardinal's Farm Clubs and Homestead, the Baseball City, but also Homestead Bayfront Park, Musselwhite Park (adult recreation exclusively), golf, the State Farmers' Market in Florida City, Everglades National Park, the Homestead Everglades Posse, Avocado Elementary School, progressive municipal government, Homestead's Modern Light Plant, "Homestead (SAC) Air Force Base, Home of the B-52s" and the Snark Missile display at the future Homestead Citizen Soldier Wayside Park. The City of Homestead emblazoned its stationary with the red St. Louis Cardinals logo.

The Cardinals left Harris Field and were replaced by the Montreal Expos. Little is known of the Expos farm system spring training at Homestead.

MISSILES AT THE READY

The special impact of the Cuban Missile Crisis, mentioned earlier, was an intense time. The crisis began in September 1962 when large shipments of Soviet military equipment were detected on the way to and within Cuba. In October 1962, the world came closer to a nuclear war than ever in history, and twenty-four Soviet medium jet bombers subsequently arrived in Cuba. When Soviet missiles were then discovered in various stages of installation, the situation became even more critical since these missiles were estimated to be able to reach almost the entire United States.

Tens of thousands of army troops and air force aircraft poured into Homestead Air Force Base. As a precaution, the B52 heavy jet bombers, equipped with nuclear weapons, were moved out. A wing of F100 Super

Army Air Defense Nike-Hercules and Hawk units that deployed from Fort Bliss, Texas, were equipped with nuclear warheads capable of shooting down Soviet enemy aircraft.

President John F. Kennedy (shown in the back seat of convertible) visited Homestead Air Force Base on November 26, 1962, to thank troops that were involved in the Cuban Missile Crisis.

Sabre jet fighters operated out of Homestead, as did F102 air defense interceptors. There was little space for the arriving troops, so most lived in tents. Local folks helped out by making sandwiches and helping feed the troops.

Equipment of all types flowed into Homestead by rail, road and air. Perhaps most significant was the deployment of an Army Air Defense Brigade from Fort Bliss, Texas. The Nike-Hercules and Hawk units were equipped with nuclear warheads capable of shooting down Soviet enemy aircraft.

After things quieted down, President John F. Kennedy visited Homestead Air Force Base on November 26, 1962, for an inspection of the units in the buildup. From the base newspaper *Alert*, we know that "an all jet flyby consisted of 72 Air Force TAC (Tactical Air Command) aircraft—F84s, F100s and F105s with two RF101 photo reconnaissance aircraft flying below them simulating the kind of low level reconnaissance that these aircraft carried out over Cuban during the Missile Crisis. Thirty-two Navy and Marine Corps A6 attack aircraft, F8 fighters and A3 bombers enhanced the all-jet fly by for President Kennedy."

The commander-in-chief was met by General Walter C. Sweeney, Commander of AFLANT (Air Force Atlantic), Major General M.A. Preston Commander of AFLANT ADVON (Advanced Command Post) and other military leaders, including Brigadier General Jack J. Catton, commander, (Homestead-based) 823rd Air Division; and Colonel Richard R. Stewart, commander, (Homestead-based) 19th Bomb Wing.

The entourage of high-level dignitaries, military heads and over one hundred press people viewed a display representative of the many aircraft and crews mustered during the buildup. At several points, the president stopped his convoy to dismount and talk to the proud airmen.

In the midst of the array of weaponry and men he halted to present the Air Force Outstanding Unit Award to the 4080th Strategic Reconnaissance Wing and 363rd Tactical Reconnaissance Wing. After pinning the streamers onto the flagstaffs, he told the group, "We are much indebted to you. We are particularly indebted to Major (Rudolf) Anderson who was a member of one of these wings who was the only casualty of the last few weeks, but who is symbolic I think of the willingness of a good many Americans to take great hazards on behalf of their country. We are very much indebted to you all." Major Anderson was a U2 pilot.

In early December, the HAFB Alert reported that the Strategic Air Command bombers and tankers had returned to Homestead and then departed "to make room for the fighters."

Just as was the case after World War II, army men and women returned to Homestead or never left after their discharge. Many were highly trained technicians whose skills easily translated to civilian jobs in South Dade.

And so it was that Homestead, like the rest of the country, breathed a sigh of relief that the Cuban Missile Crisis ended. Most had no idea of the changes that the rest of the 1960s and beyond would bring.

Chapter 6

CHANGING TIMES, INCREASING DIVERSITY

H omestead today is a very different city from the Homestead of the segregation era, a time when black people lived separately with minimal contact between the races that lasted from the coming of the railroad until almost the Civil Rights Act of 1964.

The shocking death of President John F. Kennedy in 1963 impacted Homestead strongly because he had visited the city, with all the fanfare a presidential appearance brings, only a year prior to his assassination. But that tragedy and other subsequent events occurring across the nation during the 1960s and 1970s began to impact long-held perspectives within the community. Regrettably, many of the contributions of African American residents were not officially captured in early history. As the community culture began to shift, broader public recognition of all residents came into play and the Hispanic residents also began to enjoy business and community involvement that went well beyond traditional work within the vast agricultural fields.

Notwithstanding the large number of "homesteads" that were settled in the early years, it is also worth a quick glimpse back into other land deals that were available. One of Florida's largest landowners, particularly on the East Coast, was William Gleason. A former lieutenant governor, Gleason (no relation to Jackie!) had come to Florida after the Civil War and was, for many years, active in politics and commerce on Florida's east coast. Evidence of his holdings in Homestead is shown by two letters, which are illustrated below, written at the height of the great Florida real estate boom of the 1920s. The

This letter, written to William Gleason by O.B. Ratcliffe, notes that he (Ratcliffe) could buy land close to Gleason's property for $50.00 per acre.

Opposite: A second letter from O.B. Parker, of Homestead's Alpine Groves, to Mr. Gleason, one of Florida's largest landowners.

first, written to Gleason by O.B. Ratcliffe, notes that he (Ratcliffe) could buy land close to Gleason's property for $50.00 per acre. In the second letter, O.B. Parker, of Homestead's Alpine Groves, is suggesting to Mr. Gleason that if Gleason sells his land to a Miss Miles then he (Parker) should receive some consideration. In Parker's letter, Mr. Ratcliffe is also mentioned.

And while the "complete view" of the entire populace, such as the historically important role of African American churches, may not have been routinely or officially recorded, fortunately for posterity, *Homestead*

ALPINE GROVES
O. B. PARKER, PROP.
HOMESTEAD FLORIDA

August 18th, 1925.

Mr W. H. Gleason,

Eau Gallie. Fla.

Dear Sir.

Some friends Mr & Miss Mile who are leaveing here today
for Chicago. Will call on you in the near future, In regard to your
property in Section 16 adjoining the Royal Palm Park Estate.
Miss Mile is interested in propertyes in this county. And have been
advised By Mr F. B. Ratcliffe who owns the alternate eighties in
sec 16, that you were holding your 320 acres at $ 200.00 per acre.
Which price I have quoted to Miss Mile.
In case Miss Mile should purchase your holdings in Sec 16, Will you
take care of my commission.
I am not in the Real Estate buisness. But dureing a conversation with
this party, I mentioned this tract of land, And she became interested.
Mr Gleason, was quite well acquainted with you at the time the Rail Road
was being built into Eau Gallie. As I was Conductor of work train,
when the road first entered Eau Gallie.
Trusting that the deal may consumate. And that I may have the pleasure
of meeting you again. I am,

Yours very truly.

O. B. Parker.

Then and Now, a marvelous photo-oriented booklet published by the city
in 2012 with a fine historic area map in the center features, as part of
the suggested self-guided historic tour of the city, stops at Trinity Faith
Tabernacle Deliverance Church at 512 Southwest Fourth Street and the
Greater New Mt. Zion African Methodist Episcopal Church, built in 1936,
is at 890 Southwest Fourth Street.

Homestead Then and Now noted that Trinity Faith was originally a movie
theater and cultural center, the two-story structure serving the African

American community of Homestead. The building's Masonry Vernacular architectural style maintains its artistic and architectural distinction.

Construction of the Greater New Mt. Zion African Methodist Episcopal Church was started in Homestead in 1915 with the current structure (address noted above) having been built in 1955. The church is an important edifice in the Southwest district of the city and has served the African American community through an unbroken line of thirty pastors, certainly one of the lengthiest lines of lineal descent in terms of pastoral longevity in all of Dade (later Miami-Dade) County.

According to local information, St. Paul Missionary Baptist Church was established in 1903 and became the largest African American church in Homestead, although it did not have a permanent home until 1948. For a time prior to that, there was consideration of a sanctuary being built on property donated by Mark McClain, a gentleman of historic note.

In 1927, Lawrence "Mark" McClain, a Bahamian who worked on the Florida East Coast Railway (his occupation is not noted, but he could have been a laborer, section hand, station baggage handler or, possibly, an on-train porter or dining car waiter, the latter two occupations putting him at the top of the respectability scale for black employees at the time), homesteaded 160 acres of Homestead south of Mowry Street. Splitting the property, McClain was able to turn it into McClain's Addition, and that section (160 acres is a section) was one of the first subdivisions in Homestead. McClain sold twenty-five- by seventy-five-foot lots almost exclusively to members of the black community. "McClain's Addition," one of the first subdivisions in all of South Dade County with lots of that size, became a highly desirable area in which to live.

As we have stated previously in this book, page limitations restrict us from mentioning all the notable people that we wished to include. However, several individuals must be mentioned in terms of the impact that the African American community has had on Homestead's past, present and future.

One of Homestead's pioneers in terms of longevity is Jessie Robinson Jr. Born at home in Homestead in 1935, Mr. Robinson has "seen it all" both as a younger person growing up in the city and as the revered barber, operating Robinson's Sanitary Barber Shop at 512 Southwest Sixth Avenue since 1957. Humble and gracious, Jessie is preparing to write his own history, a semi-autobiographical work that will expand on his recollections and remembrances of growing up and being a part of one of the most resilient and unique cities in America.

Although the exact dates appear to be lost in the mists of history, we do know that Clifford Hollis was the first African American police officer

Left: Roland and Eloise Buchanan with their daughter, Avis, in 1964 Homestead. The Buchanan family has seen many changes since the 1960s. *Courtesy Avis Buchanan Cooper.*

Below: Marcus Hudson's induction into the 2012 South Dade High School Concourse of Champions. Paul Worley Jr. accepted the plaque for his father, Coach Paul Worley. *Courtesy Hugh Hudson.*

in South Dade, serving both Homestead and Florida City simultaneously, according to information available at the Phicol Williams Community Center on Southwest Fourth Street.

Changes rippled throughout the community, to include transforming the schools. Men such as Coach Paul Worley of South Dade Senior High School watched the transition, and the school later cheered champions such as Marcus Hudson, who went on to be a player in the National Football League, and Super Bowl champion Antrelle Rolle, a member of the New York Giants (Super Bowl XLVI winners).

This chapter cannot be complete, of course, without mentioning and noting Homestead's first African American elected officials.

In 1975, Yvonne Brassfeld was elected the city's first black councilwoman, as was noted in an earlier chapter. It was in 1981 that Roscoe Warren became the city's first black city councilman, serving until 2001 when he became mayor. Mr. Warren then carried out his mayoral duties until 2007, and he remains interested in and active in Homestead politics and civic affairs today.

Mention must also be made of the man who has served as Homestead's chief of police since June 1998. The city's first black police chief, Alexander E. Rolle Jr., joined the force on February 29, 1980. A graduate of Barry University, Chief Rolle advanced through the ranks from patrol officer to detective, to sergeant, captain, major and then chief.

In the changing demographics of the area, the Hispanic community, too, opened many businesses and entered into public life. Again, it is not possible to single out every individual of note, yet there is a cross sample that serves the purpose of illustrating the range of contributions of families that immigrated and subsequently set down roots.

Homestead chief of police Alexander E. Rolle Jr. was a Homestead resident all of his life. Chief Rolle has been a member of the department since 1980.

The Garza family. *Left to right:* Cip Garza III, Cip Garza, Maria Garza, Eddie Garza and Alex Garza. *Courtesy the Garza family.*

Homestead's Beronnes family. *Top row, from left:* Maria, Guadalupe, Anita, Eddie, David, Cesar, Manuel, Juan, Hilda, Olga, Rosie. *Bottom row, from left:* Julio and Ignacia Beronnes. *Courtesy the Beronnes family.*

The Mexican farmworkers who came to Homestead in the early 1960s contributed not only economically but also to the social fabric of the community. A perfect example is the Garza family, who first arrived in 1963 as migrant farmworkers supporting local growers. The next generation of the Garza family all graduated from local high schools, with son Cip Garza becoming a state champion and setting records in track and field and earning his bachelors degree from University of Miami and his masters from Nova Southeastern. Today, Cip and his wife, Maria, run the Mexican-American Council, which represents that hardworking community by focusing on educational benefits for the children of farmworkers.

Another success story is the Berrones family. In 1997, Eddie Berrones became the first Mexican American member of the Homestead City Council, and he served for a period of six years. Also beginning as migrant workers, the Berrones family today owns successful businesses in the community and is active in civic affairs.

Alice Pena, the first Hispanic woman to be elected as the president of the Dade County Farm Bureau and currently serving on the board of directors, grew up on the land of PNS Farms that her parents established. As an adult, she plunged into the world of banking and international finance, traveling extensively in Central and South America, ever rising in the financial ranks. Her parents had always worked PNS Farms together, and after Pena's father passed away, she returned to her agricultural roots.

She was already well known for her decade-long advocacy for the Las Palmas Community Association, and when she lost her mother, Alice's passion to carry on their legacy came into full bloom. Her drive was funneled into not only sustaining and growing tropical fruits but also expanding into an organic egg market that is recognized with the Cornucopia Institute for Authentic Organic Egg Production's highest possible score: a Five rating.

Other families entered different businesses. Israel Marin Sr. and his wife, Sara, made a harrowing journey from Cuba, eventually settling in Homestead in 1972. They were able to afford a small home and Marin Sr. began selling clothes and jewelry out of that new home and from a van with the help of his seven-year-old son. From that beginning, they established their first stand-alone store in 1979 on Washington Avenue in Homestead. A second store was later opened on Quail Roost Drive, and with eleven years' experience in the business by the time he was only eighteen, Israel Marin, Jr. was placed in charge of the Homestead store as soon as he graduated from high school. Business continued to grow, and after Hurricane Andrew, they picked up the damaged pieces and selected their current location in the

Homestead Towne Square. They consolidated into a single store at the end of 2010, as Israel Marin, Sr. chose to semi-retire. Whether or not the third generation of Marins will become jewelers remains to be seen. Israel, Jr. and his wife, Sandy, want school to be the priority for their sons, Brandon, age twelve, and Brian, age six.

As can be seen, the rich cultural texture of present-day Homestead owes much to the families who came to the area in those early years.

At the same time as Roscoe Warren was elected to council, the city saw the election of its first Jewish mayor. While many people believe that the Greater Miami Jewish community has always been centered on and in Miami Beach, nothing could be further from the truth. Homestead has, for many years, had either one or two Jewish houses of worship (Temple Hatikvah was originally formed as a Jewish community center in 1952 and was reorganized in 1972), and in 1981, Irving Peskoe was elected to the first of three two-year terms as Homestead's highest elected official.

But the role of the Jewish community actually goes back to almost the time of the coming of the railroad. Miamian Jack Seitlin's father, Henry, who was one of the first Jewish settlers in South Florida, left Russia due to the pogroms (attacks) against the Jews by the Cossacks. Wanting to go to Palestine (Israel), he was detoured and via Philadelphia arrived in Homestead with six other Zionists late in the fall of 1909. The group planned to teach Zionists how to farm and then send them on to Palestine. While the winter of 1909–10 was delightful, the summer of 1910 was, with the influx of millions of mosquitos, brutal, and all of the men except Henry, who did not have the train fare, returned to Philadelphia. Henry, nearly penniless, moved to Miami to look for work.

Shortly thereafter, Henry brought his youngest brother, Harry, and his sister Rose down to Miami, where Rose met and married Max Lehrman. The Lehrmans then moved back down to the family's property in Homestead. Max became what was then known as a bicycle peddler and sold dry goods throughout South Dade for many years.

Although not to be considered a minority in population, the role of women in city politics must not be overlooked in Homestead's history either. In 1963, Ruth Campbell, for so long a dedicated volunteer and public servant, was elected to council for the first time. In 2007, Lynda Bell (now vice chairman of the Miami-Dade County Commission) was elected as the city's first female mayor for a two-year term. From a time when women were not even permitted to vote, few people can now imagine an all-male council!

Left: Former Homestead mayor Lynda Bell (the first female mayor of Homestead) is now vice chairman of the Miami-Dade County Commission.

Below: Chamber members Danielle Torres (Hampton Inn and Marriott), Nancy Torres (Hair Now Beauty), Raul DeLeon, (Homestead US-1 Self Storage) and Richard Erschik. *Courtesy Bonnie King-Moran.*

If, as is often shown in studies, small and medium businesses are the economic engine of a community, and the Chamber of Commerce is an integral part of the business community, then a measure of the changing Homestead can surely be seen in the membership of the Chamber of Commerce. A segment of the spectrum of businesses established in Homestead is demonstrated in the photograph on the previous page where Danielle Torres, director for sales of Hampton Inn and Courtyard Marriott, joined Nancy Torres, owner of Hair Now Beauty; Raul DeLeon, manager for Homestead US-1 Self Storage; and Richard Erschik, entrepreneur, at the monthly Chamber of Commerce networking breakfast.

While the mid-1960s through the 1980s witnessed the lessening of habitual barriers to the recognition of the diverse segments of the population, that willingness to assist friends and neighbors of any race, creed or nationality was at no time more evident than following the horror of Hurricane Andrew in 1992. In fact, many believe that although the damage caused by that vicious natural disaster was nothing short of cataclysmic, the one good thing that came from it was the fact that it brought the people of South Dade together, and that togetherness is what has allowed Homestead and the greater South Dade area to prosper as never before. The diversity among public officials and within the business community is a testament to how times have changed since the founding days of the city.

Chapter 7

SURPRISE! HOMESTEAD IS KNOWN FOR TOURISM!

In thinking about the history of a great city, one ordinarily does not equate Homestead and its surrounding area with tourism, yet that economic entity has long been an important (although perhaps overlooked) facet of the city's history.

Some may argue that Homestead really wasn't a tourist locale, but, rather, more a place to stay for the night going to or coming from the Keys, but that supposition is incorrect.

Ordinarily, in thinking about Homestead's past and much of South Dade (now Miami-Dade) County, one generally focuses on the railroad coming to and passing through the city en route to Key West and then continuing , after September 2, 1935, to Florida City. However, the single greatest revenue generator and employer for many years was agriculture and, of course, the Homestead Army Air Force Base, now the Homestead Air Reserve Base. The focus on tourism has ebbed and flowed through the years, but those efforts have sharpened in the past two decades with Homestead's growth and expanded population.

As seen in earlier chapters, there were numerous hotels, events and activities that drew some tourists to Homestead, and while not all of those withstood the natural and economic disasters that have been chronicled, the scenic beauty of the Everglades has been a constant worthy of special note.

Almost from its inception, it was recognized that the then-new Royal Palm State Park had to have some sort of lodging with room and board at an acceptable level available for travelers who chose to stay overnight at the

The exterior view of the lodge at Royal Palm State Park.

An interior view of the Royal Palm State Park lodge.

park in other than an outdoor camping mode; hence the Royal Palm Lodge was constructed. The former owner of the two images shown here noted on one of them that the date (likely the date that he or she was at the Park) was February 22, 1929. With that person's memorializing that moment in time, the reader can see exactly what the exterior of the lodge, as well as its main sitting room, looked like on that day. The copy on the back of the card is well worth revisiting: "Pleasant rooms with hot and cold water and electric lights may be had at reasonable rates. Delicious meals, special luncheons and afternoon teas are served...In preserving this wonder spot from the hand of the vandal for this and future generations your moral support and financial consideration are earnestly invited." (Your co-authors certainly concur with and heartily endorse that sentiment today!)

After the park's governance became federal, a beautiful welcome center and lodge was built at Flamingo, near Cape Sable, but was destroyed not by Hurricane Andrew but also by Hurricanes Katrina and Wilma. Built in 1959, the lodge was the only major lodging facility in the park and was closed in 2005 after being trashed by the two different hurricanes, which necessitated its demolition. A rental and tour center (which has a small souvenir shop selling those vital mosquito nets) rents kayaks and bicycles and is still in place. Additionally, there are naturalist-led boat tours through the backcountry for two hours and sailboat cruises on a fifty-foot schooner.

The lure of the Everglades may have come first, yet the beauty of Biscayne National Park (that was officially established through different governmental acts beginning in 1968) offers many programs for visitors who come to enjoy nature's abundance above and below water. The positioning of Homestead between the two parks provides a unique aspect that was, during this centennial year, recognized by a special resolution, which was approved by the Homestead City Council during the March 20, 2013 Homestead City Council meeting. The resolution designated the City of Homestead as "The Gateway to the Everglades and Biscayne National Parks."

According to the National Parks Conservation Association, recreational and eco-tourism activities related to the Everglades and Biscayne National Parks contribute millions of dollars each year to the local economies of the surrounding communities. Every year, close to one million people visit Everglades National Park and spend more than $136 million, supporting nearly two thousand local jobs in South Florida.

Additionally, the projected recreational economic impact of a restored Everglades ecosystem over the next fifty years is in excess of $16 billion for park visitation, commercial and recreational fishing and wildlife viewing

Flamingo Lodge, in Everglades National Park, at the height of its glory.

A great attraction in the beautiful Biscayne National Park is the lighthouse on Boca Chita Key, shown on December 24, 2011. *Courtesy Michael A. Downs.*

and hunting and over $46 billion when including other non-recreational economic benefits. Biscayne National Park is also a global destination that welcomes 500,000 national and international recreation visitors annually who spend more than $30 million supporting more than five hundred local jobs in South Florida.

Cycling in and around the parks and along other trails has been a longstanding source of enjoyment for residents and tourists alike. As cited in an earlier chapter, Homestead dedicated an extension of a highway for safe bicycling in 1961, although for some people, the attendance of famous actress Mae West, who thanked the City of Homestead for its efforts in supporting the sport, was the most memorable part of the ceremony. From that beginning came yet a different type of celebrity to bring attention to Homestead. Dr. Paul Dudley White, an internationally famous cardiologist and bicycle enthusiast who was previously a physician to President Dwight D. Eisenhower, founded the national-level Committee for Safe Bicycling. His interest in and advocacy for cycling led to citizens of Homestead naming the local cycling club the "Dr. Paul Dudley White Bicycle Club" in his honor. In February 1963, White dedicated the first bikeway in the United States in Homestead. The roads, as part of the street system, led from residential areas to schools, shopping centers, parks and playgrounds. Dr. White later said, "I have urged all cities to study and follow the Homestead Program. It is the perfect example of individual initiative and municipal cooperation, and demonstrates what can be accomplished at low cost and high enthusiasm."

That enthusiasm can still be seen if one is along Palm Avenue on any weekend (and many other days). Bicycles flash past as the popularity of cycling continues with numerous local clubs, frequent rides for charitable causes and events such as the annual Biscayne/Everglades Greenway Bike Festival. The forty-two-mile greenway that begins at Ernest Coe Visitor Center is currently the only one in the world that connects two national parks.

In addition to the publicity raised by the cycling popularity, more than a decade later, another series of events drew national attention to Homestead. It was the bicentennial of the United States in 1976 that saw a surge of activity in the city —some of which continues to impact the community.

Homestead was declared a Bicentennial City by the Revolutionary Bicentennial Administration, and the community responded by organizing, in that same year, the Homestead Community Concerts and the Homestead Center for the Arts, both of which have served the community ever since. The community also came together to create "Super Flag," which proudly flew over the city on special occasions and was carried in parades.

The vision for the creation of a giant United States flag to celebrate the 1976 bicentennial came from local businessman, former Homestead-Redland District Chamber of Commerce president and community activist Jack Levy in October 1975. The flag was dedicated to all veterans. Not having the convenience of the Internet in 1976, Jack and friends researched the historic dimensions of that great flag at the library and found them to be thirty feet by fifty-eight feet. The stars were twenty-two inches across, and the stripes were twenty-eight inches wide. Jack ordered 379 yards of four-ounce red, white and blue sail cloth from a supplier in Massachusetts. To that was added more than thirty thousand yards of thread.

The work was parceled out to various groups. Homestead senior citizens cut out the one hundred white stars—fifty for each side. The Homestead Power Squadron Auxiliary cut out the red and white stripes, and the women of the Royal Colonial Mobile Home Park constructed the blue field for the stars. But before any of this was done, sixteen-year old Mike Costello rinsed the material in the lake in front of City Hall at 790 North Homestead Boulevard using his rowboat. The Homestead National Guard Armory was the site where the flag pieces were joined. Most of the 150 people involved in sewing Super Flag were women. They came to call themselves the "Betsy Rosses." Like our first American flag, it was sewn by hand.

A 104-foot flagpole was erected in the Harris Field circle, which had earlier denoted the Homestead Airfield center point. The flagpole was dedicated to the late George Cooper Sr., an agricultural leader. The flag probably first flew during the Homestead-South Dade Fair.

Super Flag created much publicity for the city of Homestead, but perhaps none greater than on the Fourth of July, 1976, when 7,141 people, the largest group of new citizens ever sworn in at one time, saluted and pledged allegiance to the American Super Flag as their first act as Americans. The swearing-in ceremony took place at the Miami Beach Convention Hall with Super Flag proudly hanging as a backdrop to the stage. Millions watched on national television.

Opposite, top: Councilwoman Ruth Campbell pins a corsage on the great actress Mae West as Chamber of Commerce president Sully Adair welcomes Ms. West to Homestead in 1961.

Opposite, bottom: The Purple Martin Bicycle Festival starting in downtown Homestead, brought cyclists from across the country and around the globe.

Homestead's magnificent thirty-foot by fifty-eight-foot bicentennial flag, handmade by the city's residents.

One person can make a difference, and Jack Levy did just that while motivating more than 150 other volunteers to step forward in honoring the nation and the city. The country's bicentennial year of 1976 was indeed a proud year for Homestead!

It was in 1976, also, that local cultural leaders put their heads together and organized Homestead Community Concerts (HCC) to build a local concert audience, cultivate an interest in good music, give the public an opportunity to enjoy a minimum of three concerts and recitals yearly and foster music appreciation and the teaching of music and music history. The president was Mrs. Bruce Schaefer with John Lynn, first vice-president; Mrs. E.L. Branam, second vice-president; Mrs. James Fleming, secretary; and Lanier Porter, treasurer. Twenty-three additional board members served.

The first two years saw very high-level performers grace the stage at South Dade High School. They included classical pianist and Julliard faculty member Rudolph Firkusky, Fred Waring & the All New Young Pennsylvanians, Roberta Peters of the Metropolitan Opera in New York, operatic baritone Theodor Uppman, the Romaros Guitar Quartet, Roger Wagner Chorale and the Oslo Philharmonic. HCC has become accustomed to being rated the top organization in its grant category by the Miami-Dade Cultural Affairs Council. Its 2013 president is Red McAllister, who is a retired Miami-Dade public schools chief of police.

Within the efforts to advance cultural and artistic offerings, the Homestead Center for the Arts was also formed in 1976. Its purpose was to establish a permanent nonprofit facility to house and promote cultural interests associated with the arts. Ed Ghezzi, a generous local architect, drew up plans for the single-story auditorium pro-bono, and HCA began an aggressive fundraising effort.

Officers were: Marion Archer, president; Mike Gallagher, first vice-president; Ginny Munz, second vice-president; Dorothy Jones, recording secretary; Dorothy Douglas, corresponding secretary; and Alice Rhyne, treasurer. Twenty-four additional directors served.

HCA also explored working jointly with Miami-Dade College Homestead Campus to restore existing theater buildings but could not overcome the estimated cost of operating a facility without government subsidy.

Today, HCA sponsors the Bea Peskoe Lunchtime Lecture Series, provides scholarships to college students from the community majoring in the arts, acts as an umbrella organization for local arts organizations and supports the arts in any way possible. The Miami-Dade County Cultural Affairs Council funds a grant program administered by HCA to support small local arts groups because Homestead has been historically underserved by other existing cultural organizations.

As with so many aspects of life in the area, venues for arts and culture were severely impacted by the devastation of Hurricane Andrew and in helping restore both the past and future sense of history, arts and culture, the Homestead Historic Preservation Board worked diligently with multiple organizations and agencies to obtain approval for downtown Homestead to be designated in the National Registry of Historic Places. This was achieved in 2007, and among the many efforts to highlight the historical look of Krome Avenue, the Rotary Club was key in replanting the iconic palms that were often featured in old photographs.

Homestead and its environs featured (and in most cases still offer) a number of other welcoming attractions, including the Rare Bird Farm, Monkey Jungle, the Fruit and Spice Park, Camp Owaissa-Bauer, Coral Castle, Homestead Bayfront Park, the Pioneer Museum in Florida City, the Redland Trail and more. Hotels and restaurants have expanded significantly,

Above: Homestead Bayfront Park is a beautiful setting for swimming, lounging and relaxing and is complete with locker facilities and snack bar.

Left: Tourists and residents alike enjoy making the ten stops designated along the historic Redland Tropical Trail that moves in and out of Homestead.

and RV parks have long been a popular means for visitors to appreciate the area. At certain times of the year, of course, the major tourist attraction is the Homestead-Miami Speedway, the story of which is closely tied to the devastating Hurricane Andrew that impacted the lives of all and forever changed the lives of many.

Chapter 8

HURRICANE ANDREW

Homestead Before and After

I t was *not,* as the expression goes, "a day like all other days." In fact, August 24, 1992 was a day that has lived in infamy in South Florida.

In reporting on and discussing the brutality of Hurricane Andrew, it should be noted that a number of sources were used herein, including stories that appeared in the *Miami Herald, Sun-Sentinel, New York Times, TIME* magazine, *U S. News and World Report, Newsweek Magazine* and several publications dealing with the storm including *Hurricane Survival Guide 2002,* published by WESH Channel Two and the *Orlando Sentinel,* its sub-title being *Andrew: 10 Years Later.* That magazine-type piece is a fine retrospective on that terrible blow. Because there is so much "out there," and with the authors recognizing the importance of avoiding even a hint of plagiarism in their writing, a disclaimer is necessary in this chapter: the reader is advised that because there are so many sources of information on and about Hurricane Andrew, and because so much of the information and material proffered is essentially, in many cases, the same or close thereto, a general attribution, for the edification of the reader, was made at the start of this paragraph.

Most of August 1992 had been a typical Florida summer month: hot and muggy with afternoon showers most days. Although the hurricane season begins on June 1, and even though there have been early-season hurricanes, Floridians know that, for the most part, August and September, with an occasional early to mid-October storm, are the "normal" months for hurricanes, with a November happening being a fairly rare event. Until August 23 of '92, August had been a "normal" month.

Life was going on as it usually does in Homestead and everywhere else in the world. In fact, in early August, co-author Bramson and his wife spent a marvelously enjoyable day in the city antiquing the numerous shops then thriving in the downtown area and enjoying a terrific lunch at Tiffany's. Unquestionably, the finds that day were excellent, including some early Florida City material, several great early Homestead pieces and a few very nice FEC Railway items that we had not seen before. It was really a good day!

While not changing our view of how terrific that particular day was, Hurricane Andrew changed almost everything else. Several sources have estimated that the storm caused more than $25.3 billion in damage in the state of Florida alone. Bryan Norcross of Miami's Channel Four and other meteorologists stated that, had the storm been slightly larger or made landfall a few miles farther north, it would have significantly affected Miami and Fort Lauderdale, which would have resulted in a damage and death toll almost incalculably higher. But the path of the storm was disastrous enough as it took Andrew only a few hours to blast its devastating swath across Southeast Florida, leaving hundreds of thousands homeless and a toll on the psyche of so many that the damage remains, even today, incalculable as the storm reduced once-comfortable suburban sprawl to a trail of rubble.

According to the September 7, 1992 issue of *Newsweek Magazine*, "the storm splintered houses, flattened cars, toppled trees and whipped power lines around like children's jump ropes...At the weekend, 22 people had died as a result of the storm, many crushed to death in their own homes."

Although there were thousands of photographs made of the destruction and devastation caused by Hurricane Andrew following the storm, very few images showed the human suffering and the toll that the storm took on the people who survived it. For its September 7, 1992 cover photograph, *Newsweek Magazine* chose an image of a young Homestead couple, who, having made it through a night of terror, are clinging to each other, standing in the remains of the home they once occupied, happy just to be alive.

Once the storm was over, dazed victims stumbled from the remains of once-lovely homes and apartment houses (most of the trailers and mobile homes in the storm's path were reduced to kindling wood, crumpled metal and splinters, not even recognizable as once having been human habitats) into streets without numbers or name signs, so covered by debris as to create a sense of being lost on an alien world. Clothing, household goods, toys, the remains of furniture and appliances and pieces of what must have been, up until the day of the storm, dwellings were scattered over a miles-wide area, leaving victims with little to no hope of resuming a normal life at any time

The cover of the September 7, 1992 *Newsweek Magazine* showed a young Homestead couple standing in the remains of their home following Hurricane Andrew, just happy to be alive. *Courtesy Homestead Historic Town Hall Museum.*

in a beyond-determinate "near" future. Pets—those which survived—were as dazed and bewildered as their owners, and many simply wandered about neither comprehending what had happened or aware of what their future might be.

Tom Matthews and Peter Katel wrote in *Newsweek*, "Many were without food or water and federal aid was slow in coming." And one local official demanded to know, in frustration, "where the hell the cavalry is on this one." Others pleaded with county and state officials for assistance, saying, "We need food, we need water, we need shelter and we need people."

Cadres of volunteers built temporary roofs so residents could move back into their homes even though, in some cases, they would be water- and power-less for several months to come. As one resident noted, "They were like angels from on high; we had no place else to go and at least we could stay in our own houses—as difficult as it was—and protect what little we still had."

The volunteers also cleared debris, repaired windows and removed water-soaked carpets. With little time for sleep, some of the volunteer groups helped salvage more than twenty homes in as many days.

In looking back at what was a life-changing event for the area, on August 23, 2012, Greg Allen, reporting for National Public Radio, presented a retrospective of the hurricane in which he stated that, adjusted for inflation, the August 1992 storm was, after Katrina, the second-costliest storm in U.S. history. At the same time, it also changed how forecasters report on and respond to hurricanes.

"Andrew," Allen said, "hit in a hurricane season that had started out as uncharacteristically quiet." Max Mayfield, a former forecaster at the National Hurricane Center and now a hurricane expert for the Weather Channel told Allen that he remembered receiving calls from reporters throughout July and August asking where the storms were. He answered, Allen reported, by telling them to "keep your fingers crossed that it stays that way."

Bryan Norcross, former chief meteorologist for Miami's Channel Four and now with Mayfield at the Weather Channel, has revisited the storm numerous times and never hesitates to talk about how horrific it was. When Andrew formed in the Atlantic in mid-August, it was a weak storm that many thought would fall apart. It really didn't become a hurricane until August 22, which was only two days before it struck South Florida on the twenty-fourth. None of the forecast models of the time predicted that Andrew would become a major storm at least until several days later, on Saturday.

Andrew hit the Bahamas as a Category Five hurricane on the Saffir-Simpson Hurricane wind scale, which is the top and worst possible level, indicating sustained winds of more than 157 miles per hour. At Category Five, a high percentage of framed homes will be destroyed, with total roof failure and wall collapse. Fallen trees and power poles will isolate residential areas, and power outages will last for weeks to possibly months. Most of the area will be uninhabitable for weeks or months. As the hurricane barreled toward South Florida, most residents had less than a day to prepare their homes and to evacuate coastal areas.

On the morning of August 24, Andrew slammed into the Florida coast, approximately thirty to thirty-five miles south of downtown Miami. On WTVJ (Channel Four), Norcross was able, thanks to the station's emergency generators, to stay on the air as Andrew blasted, battered and decimated the region. He was indefatigable, catching short catnaps and telling residents within the Channel Four viewing/listening area to retreat to the safest room in the house (usually a bathroom or a closet) and protect themselves with and by getting under mattresses.

The storm's wind speeds were later estimated to be above 160 miles per hour; gauges used to measure the wind's velocity first broke and then blew away under the storm's relentless pounding. As terrible as it was, Andrew was a comparatively small and fast-moving storm, tiny in size compared to the slow-moving monsters such as the more recent storms Katrina and Rita. But along with 1969's Hurricane Camille and the terrible Labor Day 1935 hurricane, Andrew was only the third Category Five hurricane to make landfall in the continental United States since records were first kept.

One of those with firsthand knowledge of the storm is Douglas Austin. He, with his wife, in-laws and one-year-old son, elected to remain and to take their chances and ride out the storm. Austin told NPR's Greg Allen that he thought that it was around quarter of five in the morning when a plank from his neighbor's fence came crashing through his bedroom window. With glass flying everywhere, he packed the entire family into a hallway closet. It appeared that they could ride out the storm there, but for whatever reason, his father-in-law decided to open the house's front door, which, as Austin said, "was a terrible mistake."

"When the wind caught the front door," Austin recalled, "it almost blew it off the hinges. Even worse, the wind was so strong that as it roared through the house, it knocked down a majority of the interior walls."

Because Austin's home was built of concrete block ("CBS" construction), the exterior walls remained standing, but his roof was gone and the interior was completely devastated. Counting themselves lucky to be alive, the Austins left the house and saw that almost all of their neighbors had suffered similar damage. Cars were battered if not destroyed by concrete debris coming from all directions, and it looked, according to survivors, as if a series of bombs had gone off, the explosions devastating everything in sight.

As people emerged into the now again sunny landscape and began to assess the damage, it was obvious that the amount of devastation differed substantially from neighborhood to neighborhood.

Allen, in his report, said that the houses in Austin's neighborhood were only a few years old but that nearly all had suffered severe damage. Some other neighborhoods saw little more than downed trees, some broken windows or missing shingles, but that really was a function of how far north they were relative to the eye of the storm. In many cases, the difference in damage was also related to how the homes were built, the materials used, the quality of the workmanship and the adherence to a nowhere-near-as-strong-as-it-should-have-been hurricane building code.

Ricardo Alvarez, a researcher who specializes in hurricane protection, stated that Andrew was mostly a wind issue, with not that much rain, and was actually a "wake-up call" to the people living in hurricane-prone regions. While the building code existed, the problem, Alvarez said, was that investigators inspecting the damage found many of the problems were caused by faulty construction, the county having allowed builders to use cost-saving shortcuts such as weaker-than-required strand board instead of heavy plywood and using either staples or one-penny nails to hold the roofs in place instead of roofing nails.

Although one of the builders' associations fought improvements in the hurricane code, county and city officials banned the use of both staples and strand board. Mr. Alvarez helped to develop an extremely strong nail that has since become the standard for all roof construction in South Florida. In addition, the region's building code now requires all homes covered by wind storm insurance to have up-to-date storm shutters or impact-resistant glass, and all doors must now open outward rather than inward. Thanks to Hurricane Andrew, South Florida has the strongest building code in the nation.

The storm, as all hurricanes do, mercifully passed over the area and came to an end, but the complete and utter feeling of hopelessness and despair was both widespread and pervasive. Thousands of families left for "points north" from Broward County to other states, with many choosing not to return. And yet, as they had so many times in the past when the going had gotten tough, the tough got going.

City officials pleaded for state and federal assistance, and slowly but surely that help came. From Florida state troopers patrolling the streets to prevent looting to federal funds, a great but temporarily bruised and beaten-up city began to come back to life. As part of the recovery efforts following the hurricane, Joint Task Force Andrew was assembled by the military and included multiple organizations brought from around the country. Logistical and engineering units remained in the area for weeks after the initial support effort began.

Prior to their arrival, however, on the day after Hurricane Andrew, the Homestead Mennonite Church put out a call for volunteers to the Mennonite Central Committee and the Mennonite Relief Committee in Lancaster, Pennsylvania. Precepts of the Mennonite faith include tithing, ongoing community service and, particularly, disaster relief efforts. Modern Mennonites of the United States responded to the call from Hurricane Andrew with dollars and volunteers, and those resources were all directed to Homestead. The local church kept a food kitchen open for eighteen months, feeding anyone who showed up. Forty volunteers a month, on a rotating basis, fueled a rebuilding campaign—first for congregants and their neighbors and later for anyone who needed help. Carpenters and roofers especially were recruited from congregations and also from the local community. Shipments of scarce materials were organized for delivery to Homestead. When the Homestead community appeared able to continue renewal, after twenty-four months, the church quietly shifted its work elsewhere in the nation. No recognition of its labor mobilization was made; none was expected.

Specifically as a result of the Hurricane Andrew relief work, the Mennonite Central Committee reformed its international relief structure, rewrote its template for disaster response and opened regional offices to speed supplies and workers where they are most needed. In 2012, the Homestead Rotary Club officially presented a public thank-you for the Hurricane Andrew relief efforts to the local Mennonite church and its then-leader, Elder Rick Lee.

With 2012 being the twentieth anniversary since Hurricane Andrew tore through the city, the *South Dade News Leader*, the stalwart community paper that has been a part of Homestead for nearly a century itself, published a special edition as people recalled those difficult days, weeks and months. Local businesses were all affected in some way or the other, and while only a small sampling of those stories could be included due to page limitations of this book, they speak to the range of impact of not only that day but also of the struggle that followed.

The procedures and equipment of Blaylock Oil Company, at 724 South Flagler Avenue, have changed over the decades, but not its commitment to fair value and taking care of customers. A Homestead business since 1965, Hayden Blaylock knew the business and his customers and friends, and that was perhaps never more evident than during Hurricane Andrew when the area reeled from the destruction, electrical power not fully restored for months. Blaylock Oil sustained minor damage, although a twenty-foot steel beam that was torn from one building was hurled such a long distance that it was never found.

Blaylock understood the urgent needs of the devastated region, and his company was operating the next day, with crucial oil and fuel being delivered to run generators that became lifelines for so many people. Blaylock opened his gates to allow army units to set up refueling operations, and when one of his vendors in South Carolina shipped him three generators, he was able to widen his range of support. Those in Homestead who watched the Miami Dolphins play in the aftermath of Hurricane Andrew were able to do so partially because Blaylock Oil Company was providing fuel to their generators. The University of Miami, Florida Atlantic University and other institutions were on that list as well.

Suzanne Dalton's father-in-law, Ronald, and her husband, Jeff, jointly opened Dalton Marine Supply on South Dixie Highway in 1987. They built a loyal clientele among commercial fishermen and also leisure boaters, many of whom were stationed at Homestead Air Force Base. They were known for their boating expertise and ability to quickly order and receive parts they didn't carry. "No one was really predicting that Andrew was going to hit us," Dalton said. "My family has an annual family reunion in the Keys, and we were down there. When they evacuated the Keys, we came up and started preparing." When they initially opened the solidly built concrete store, they decided to invest in sliding hurricane shutters. While that did protect the windows and doors, power lines came down, wrapping around part of the building, and when the rooftop air conditioning system was ripped away, the hole allowed water to flood in. "We were fortunate though because our small house in Homestead was concrete with tongue-and-groove interior. My mother, aunt and neighbors lost everything," she said. "We came to the store, cleaned up what we could, secured things and then focused on our families."

Dalton described the weeks without power or telephones. "I never imagined having to stand in line in a food tent, but what else can you do?" Dalton took other relatives' children in with her young ones to free up the adults to try and arrange new homes or repairs. A plastic swimming pool became the laundry and bathtub as their store was partially open during mostly daylight hours. That set up a "chicken and egg" situation. Without full capability in the store, their primary source of revenue was gone. In a business like Dalton Marine, there is a constant flow of inventory coming in and going out. One of the last things on anyone's mind was leisure boating, and the commercial fishermen had lost many of their boats. "You learn how to make do, to cut expenses until you can get back on your feet," Dalton said quietly. "We had good insurance, and they didn't drop our home, but the commercial insurer notified us after they paid the claim that they were no longer insuring commercial properties. We did find a new carrier," she added.

Andy Fischer and Sons Jewelry and Gifts has been in Homestead since the 1950s. "The store was pretty well demolished," Fischer said. "The exterior walls, roof and floor were a mess." The Fischers faced the same choice as did so many other business owners: quit or rebuild. This was home though, and despite the upheaval, they set about to build a new store on Northwest Fourteenth Street, knowing that the chaos heaped on Krome Avenue was not likely to be quickly overcome.

"We were in and open by Christmas," Fischer recalled, with slight changes to their inventory. The tablewares of china, silver and crystal went by the wayside, but jewelry, watches, clocks, artwork and other gifts remained.

In 1919, Wilfred J. Vick and his wife, Edith, came to Homestead from Ohio and began farming on an original twenty acres. The second generation grew up with the land, and then the third generation joined in the family business that even incorporated crop-dusting for a number of years. At the peak of their farming, the Vicks owned close to four hundred acres and leased other acreage. Agriculture is a dynamic business, however, and in 1980, Fred and his brother Mike established Vick Farms Palms. The palm and ornamental plant business continued to prosper, and in 1988, Gary, Fred's other brother, and their cousin Walter entered into the venture. In 1990, they moved out of traditional produce and expanded the tree farm. Prior to that transition, Tommy, Wilfred's four-year-old son, became the fourth generation of Vicks to take to the land. "I think I still hold the record as the youngest-ever person to open an account at the bank we used," he said with a smile.

Tommy was nine years old when Hurricane Andrew hit, knocking over virtually every tree in the nursery. Notwithstanding his young age, Tommy ran the crew repotting plants in the nursery as up to 150 or more people worked for almost three months setting the trees upright and stabilizing them so they could re-root.

Ron Webb, a member of one of the early families in Homestead and owner of Homestead Furniture, explained the essence of the damage wrought by the hurricane. If you had gone shopping for new furniture on Saturday, August 22, 1992, at Homestead Furniture on Krome Avenue, you could have strolled through six showrooms in four different buildings. If there was something you wanted that you didn't see, perhaps they had it in their nearby warehouse. On that following Monday, Hurricane Andrew tore away the third floor of the Horne Building, crashing it through the roof of one of the Homestead Furniture buildings. "I've lived here all my life, and that morning, I didn't recognize where I was. Trees and familiar landmarks had simply disappeared," Ron Webb said.

When he did make it to Krome Avenue, it was to find his buildings with gaping holes, inventory in the showrooms destroyed or soaked. "That was what kept me from being looted the ways others were," Webb explained. "What good was wet furniture?" He, like most owners, quickly armed against robbery. "Police cars and fire trucks had been destroyed. If you could get out, nails in chunks of wood littered the roads, puncturing tires, and who had gas?" Webb summed up the dire situation. "It was a life-changing event for everyone. There was no normal—the Homestead we knew was gone. No power, no telephones, no gas, no money, no effective police and fire protection and ice was like gold—it was like living in a third-world country." With the warehouse being the least damaged, he began to work out of it with what inventory he had, primarily filling Red Cross vouchers. It was a difficult task in the August and September heat with no power.

Webb's furniture business was one thing—his forty-nine rental properties were another matter. "Forty-one were total losses," he said. Although insurance covered much of his inventory, that was not the case for his multiple buildings. As the recovery process languished, exacerbated by the closure of the air force base, Webb sold many of his holdings and downsized to the current store devoted to antiques and collectibles.

Webb's summation is perhaps the quintessential statement of that terrible day. "In the space of two hours, everything changed. People who went through Andrew mark their lives as how things were before or after the storm."

At the ten-year mark after Hurricane Andrew, a jointly produced *Orlando Sentinel* and WESH Channel Two's 2002 "Hurricane Survival Guide" was developed with the cover showing a survivor, barefooted and bereft of anything other than the pants that he had on during the storm. This image brings the pathos and sorrow of the aftermath of that storm home even harder than most words can convey.

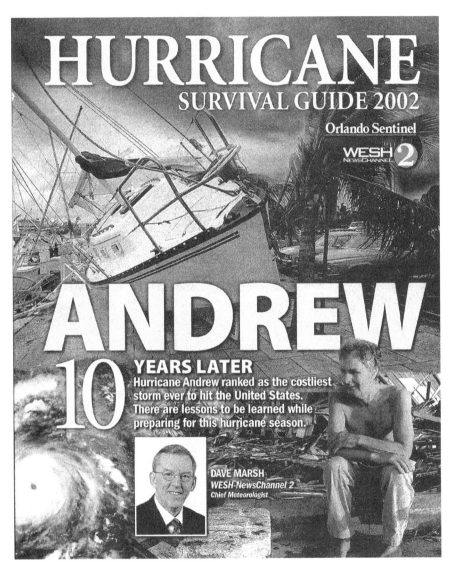

The cover of the jointly produced *Orlando Sentinel* and WESH Channel 2's 2002 "Hurricane Survival Guide" is shown here.

As hard as it may be to believe, this is what the area that would become the Homestead-Miami Speedway looked like in 1958.

And so it was that even as the physical recovery began, the economic struggles were not well understood beyond the immediate area. Long-term assistance would be needed, and an economic boost came in September 1992, barely one month after Hurricane Andrew left its trail of destruction. Longtime Miami motorsports promoter Ralph Sanchez, working with then Homestead city manager Alex Muxo, was able to negotiate a deal that was approved quickly by the city council to build a facility that would begin the revitalization of the city. It should be noted that while the story of the Speedway is significant, Ruth Campbell was a strong, initial voice in urging Ralph Sanchez to build the speedway.

A site was selected, an area that in 1958 had been photographed with several groves and fewer roads visible, not even half a dozen houses to be seen. Few looking at it would have envisioned it as anything other than agricultural land. However, on August 24, 1993, groundbreaking took place for the 434-acre facility that would be known as Homestead-Miami Speedway

Above: The completed
1.5-mile racetrack at
Homestead-Miami
Speedway with the
inaugural race, the Jiffy
Lube 300, in November
1995.

Left: This is the cover of
the elaborate program
published for the 1998
Miami Grand Prix Race
held at Homestead-Miami
Speedway.

(HMS). Businessman H. Wayne Huizenga became a partner in the project prior to completion.

Two years later, on November 3, 1995, grand-opening ceremonies for the Speedway were held, and NASCAR debuted in front of a sold-out crowd. Executives and dignitaries were given the honor of cutting the ribbon, following which Dale Jarrett won the November 5 Jiffy Lube Miami 300. On November 4, former Daytona 500 champion Geoffrey Bodine became the Speedway's first race winner in a NASCAR Craftsman Truck Series exhibition race. In a contrast both to the previous photo showing the approximate location of the Homestead-Miami Speedway in 1958 and those showing the terrible destruction of Hurricane Andrew, this image conveys one word to the stricken area: hope.

By 1998, the yearly Grand Prix was a major American and worldwide racing event, bringing in the top names from racing from throughout the world and continuing to help Homestead to recover from the terrible trauma of six years earlier. That year, the then-named Marlboro Grand Prix sponsored by Toyota Races of March 13–15 presented race-goers with a 148-page monster of a book, complete with information, history, ads and details of the races. Each year's program becomes more elaborate and, incredibly, in most years, larger than the issue of the previous year. Although the Grand Prix is no longer run at Homestead, there are many racing and motorsports events conducted throughout the year. The largest series of events take place each November when the final races of the NASCAR season are run to the delight of millions of viewers worldwide.

NASCAR president Mike Helton credits Sanchez with adapting to the stock car sanctioning body's needs in various track modifications in the initial years and making Homestead-Miami "a very significant destination for NASCAR and its fans."

"Ralph certainly believed in the original [relatively flat and rectangular] design of Homestead, but he also was willing to make adjustments to accommodate the sanctioning bodies," Helton said. "He always delivered on what he was trying to accomplish."

As a note to the memory of the man who brought world-renowned racing to Homestead, Sanchez died after a long battle with cancer on April 1, 2013, at the age of sixty-four.

Notwithstanding the projected economic boost of the Speedway, in 1993 the Homestead Main Street organization was also formed to seek and infuse funding from other sources. It was instrumental in bringing state and federal grants to rebuild the downtown business district. Main

Street worked with the City, merchants and cultural groups to upgrade and promote downtown and continues to do so through conducting numerous special events and sponsoring other projects.

Above all, it should be emphasized that while physical recovery efforts started quickly and progress was made in many areas, the economic recovery was prolonged and, at times, quite painful for well more than a decade. Those who remained in Homestead through the full aftermath of recovery are the modern bedrock of the post-Andrew Homestead.

Chapter 9

OUR FRIENDS AND NEIGHBORS

Homestead is, simply put, "the capital" of south Miami-Dade County. With its close neighbor, Florida City, adjoining it to the south, Homestead is really the hub of an area stretching from Cutler Bay and the Redland down to Florida City's southern border and on to Monroe County's Key Largo.

The original Homestead Air Force Base was once located several miles to the northeast of Homestead, but due to annexation of formerly unincorporated land immediately to the east and northeast of the original city limits during the late-1990s, the city and the far southwestern perimeter of the (now) Homestead Air Reserve Base share a common border for a small portion along Southwest 137th Avenue (Speedway Boulevard).

Greater Homestead, however, encompasses a much larger area than that discussed above. Beginning on the north with the town of Cutler Bay, the Homestead metro area stretches south to the south boundary of Florida City. Although not within that geographic area, the Florida Power and Light Company Turkey Point Nuclear Plant maintains a Homestead mailing address.

Cutler Bay came into existence in January 2005, when the residents of what would become known as Cutler Bay voted to incorporate. What is now Cutler Bay was once part of Cutler Ridge, which was where the early Homestead settlers had to travel in order to purchase supplies.

South of Cutler Bay is part of the original unincorporated area of Goulds. The area that became Goulds was settled in 1900 by homesteaders. According to several sources, Goulds received its name when the Florida

Shown during the Key West Extension era, this view of the FEC depot in Goulds was taken circa 1921.

East Coast Railway built a siding in 1903, operated by an employee of the railroad named Lyman Gould. It was first known as Gould's Siding and later shortened to Goulds. The railroad depot was located near the current Southwest 216th Street.

Many packinghouses were built along Old Dixie Highway, and with those came several saloons that served the population of itinerant field workers. Although many of the packinghouses were destroyed by a tornado in 1919 or severely damaged by the 1926 Miami hurricane, a number of them were rebuilt and remained in business until the late 1960s.

The downtown area had a post office, a grocery store and an apartment building, but much of the former downtown area is now a part of the Cauley Square shops, a lovely shopping and dining complex at the center of today's Goulds. In addition, the talented Goulds Church of Christ Singers, led by Elder Edward Gooding, were an integral part of *The Homestead Story*, a production that was presented at the February 2, 2013 Centennial Celebration of Homestead at Harris Field Pavilion.

The next unincorporated area to the south is Princeton. As a small town and depot along the Florida East Coast Railway in the 1900s, the community was named by Gaston Drake, owner of Drake Lumber Company, for his alma mater, Princeton University. Many of the town buildings were even painted the school's colors of black and orange. Drake operated a sawmill and lumber company in Princeton supplying Miami, the Florida Keys and Cuba until the local timber gave out in 1923. Princeton is a very heavily ethnically mixed community with a population in 2000 of approximately ten thousand people.

Naranja is the next community south of Princeton. One of Naranja's—and, indeed, South Florida's—foremost attractions is the mysterious Coral Castle, built by a European immigrant by the name of Ed Leedskalnin in memory of his lost love. On South Dixie Highway at approximately 288th Street (technically, just a few blocks south of Naranja, but with all advertising referring to its location as Naranja), the Coral Castle's construction remains a mystery and the subject of speculation as most visitors wonder how Mr. Leedskalnin moved the huge blocks of rock to build the attraction. Ed single-handedly carved over 1,100 tons of coral rock, and his unknown process has created one of the world's most mysterious accomplishments. Having done his work only at night, nobody ever saw the actual feat taking place. As a note, the original sculptures were built in 1920 in Florida City until Ed moved them to the current location, where he continued his extraordinary deeds until 1951.

Modello, just north of Homestead, was settled fairly early in the twentieth century. In 1922, Modello pioneer S.A. Murden sent a letter and a promotional piece extolling Modello's virtues. Although a good bit of that sale sheet does talk about the Miami area in general, one can see in the image that it is primarily a vehicle for selling Modello as an ideal spot to live and farm.

Florida City, just south of Homestead, is the southernmost municipality in the South Florida metropolitan area and is the southernmost city in the United States that is not on an island. In 2000, the city's estimated population was 7,843, and as of 2004, the population estimated by the U.S. Census Bureau was 8,363. Florida City is also the last stop on the mainland before embarking on Highway U.S. 1 toward the Florida Keys. The southern terminus of the Homestead Extension of Florida's Turnpike, where it ends at its junction with U.S. 1, is located in Florida City. The city actually originated as a land promotion named Detroit. There were no buildings in the area when the first thirty families arrived from what was not yet "the motor city" in 1910, and they had to stay in Homestead until their houses could be built. The name was changed to Florida City when the town incorporated in 1914. It has a small historic area, but the city is also known for its hotels, motels, restaurants and other tourist facilities.

MODELLO

DADE COUNTY   FLA.

is on the Key West extension of the Florida East Coast Railway, at the extreme end of the peninsula, 25 miles below MIAMI, 392 miles below Jacksonville. Daily trains and mails.

ROADS. The east coast of Florida is noted for the hard rock roads. The National Automobile Association have for several years had an annual meet at Ormond, on the east coast, and there more than one world's record has been broken and a new one made which stands to-day.

MODELLO is only a few miles from either the ocean or Gulf of Mexico, and is down almost on the extreme end of the Florida peninsula. Constant breezes keep the air cool in summer, while the proximity of the large bodies of water —Lake Okeechobee on the north—temper the northwest winds of winter and render them balmy and pleasant. OURS IS THE IDEAL WINTER RESORT OF ALL NORTH AMERICA, while our summers are pleasant. Our highest temperature rarely, if ever, exceeds 92 degrees, and our lowest winter mark 46 degrees.

THE LAND. The surface of the country is of a coral rock formation and the soil is a very rich clay-like loam. The most wonderful crop of winter and early spring vegetables are raised here. Nearly a million dollars have been made by our truckers on a tomato crop in a single season, while the fruit crop is enormous.

TIMBER. The entire section is covered with pine timber, not large, but tall and straight. Valuable for mill purposes.

FRUITS. The oranges, grape fruit, lemon, lime, mango, avacado or alligator pear., sapadillo, pineapple, guava and coccanut grow to perfection, while peaches fruit in one or two years and are earlier by three weeks in Northern market than from any other section. Strawberries can be shipped in January and do well.

POULTRY do well, require but little attention, and pay well.

HEALTH. The country is perfect, healthy, and fevers and malaria are unknown

WATER is pure and abundant.

MODELLO is a new section, just opened up by the new railroad which is being built by Mr. H. M. Flagler, out to sea 156 miles from Miami to Key West. This railroad will be completed by January, 1910, and will be the most wonderful in the world, no such engineering feat ever having been attempted. In fact, some of the most noted engineers of both Europe and America pronounced it impossible, but the most difficult portion has been built, at the cost of millions of dollars, and it will be completed without unreasonable delay. Trains now run through to Knights Key, 100 miles further south, and there connect with commodious steamers for Key West and Havana, Cuba.

CLIMATE. The summer climate is mild and pleasant. The winter climate does not require mention.

STOCK AND FARMING. This is not a stock country, nor is general farming carried on. In the warmer weather our people do little work of any kind.

FENCES. This is by law a no fence country.

LANDS AND CLEARING. Lands can be bought for purposes of actual settlement at from $25.00 to $75.00 per acre— 10 acres will make an ideal fruit farm and home. THERE IS NO LAND FOR SALE AT THIS PLACE to speculators. Homeseekers only need apply. To clear the land for tree planting costs from $30 to $50 per acre. Lands will never be low priced on the east coast of Florida.

The undersigned will answer all letters that enclose a stamp.

Sincerely,

S. A. MURDEN,

Modello, Dade Co., Fla.

Above: This is a 1922 letter (on the other side of this promotional piece) that Modello pioneer S.A. Murden sent extolling Modello's virtues.

Opposite, top: The Princeton depot of the FEC Railway is shown while still in service, circa 1964, with South Dixie Highway in the background.

Opposite, bottom: The intriguing and unique Coral Castle is one of Florida's most popular tourist sites.

139

A. C. L. R. R. Depot, Palm Ave.,
Florida City, Fla.

FLORIDA CITY POLICE DEPARTMENT

CALL
25
DAY or NIGHT
Marshal's Home Phone
1418

FLORIDA CITY FIRE DEPARTMENT

Fire Call
343

Above: Incredible view, circa 1921,
of Palm Avenue looking west
toward the FEC depot. This view
actually was printed with the
wrong railroad's initials on it.

Left: Early Florida City emergency
information for residents. Note the
two-, three- and four-digit numbers
on the card.

Visitors today do not always realize when they have crossed the city limits between Homestead and Florida City, yet the town once named Detroit provides big-box stores as well as small businesses and services. Mayor Otis Wallace, a graduate of Michigan State University, earned his Juris Doctor degree from the University of Miami in 1977. Serving five years with the Dade County Public Defender's office and since 1984 in private practice, Mayor Wallace ran for and was elected to the Florida City Commission and then, in 1984, was elected mayor of the city that he has served faithfully since.

And what about the Redland?

Sometimes incorrectly pluralized as "The Redlands," the region was traditionally a mostly agricultural community. In the last several years, however, as with much of the rest of South Dade County, large homes are being built in the area, as much for the new owners to enjoy the semi-rural environment as to get away from the "big city" hustle, bustle, hubbub and crowds. Many farms, original clapboard homes of early settlers, u-pick 'em fields and coral rock walls still dot the landscape, however. Redland is named for the red clay that dominates the area, on top of a massive layer of oolitic rock. Early residents intentionally created the singular community name "Redland" to make it easier for those interested to differentiate the town from Redlands, California.

It should be noted here that much of the information in this section dealing with the Redland comes from the several "Redland District" booklets that are part of the Bramson Archive.

Redland originated in anticipation of the arrival of Henry Flagler's Florida East Coast Railway when pioneer homesteaders in the early 1900s developed a way of working the difficult soil, called scarifying or plow-breaking. This revolutionary method of agriculture allowed the land there to develop into the "winter greenery basket of America" and the "garden capital of the world." The center of town was located near Redland Road and Bauer Drive. Redland has been a source of amazement to agriculturalists, botanists and naturalists around the world, including John James Audubon and David Fairchild, both of whom spent time there.

Today, with so many newcomers moving into the area, some are referring to it as the "New Hamptons," since there are many people from northern states buying property and establishing residences in the area.

According to the online publication "About the Redland" by Karen Harris, many houses built in the area must be on a minimum of five acres of land, a law put into place to thwart development and preserve the area.

Florida City's mayor Otis Wallace, elected in 1984 and still serving the city's residents in that capacity.

Within the area there are still many groves of various types, and peacocks live abundantly and freely within the groves. Redland has also been designated a wild bird sanctuary. (Ms. Harris does not document which jurisdiction has put the five-acre minimum tract law in place, but it likely is either the County Commission, the Homestead City Council or both.)

With its subtropical climate, many tropical fruit crops are grown in the Redland that cannot be grown commercially elsewhere in the United States (outside of Southern Florida) including, among others, mango, avocado, guava, passion fruit, lychee, jack fruit, canistel, sapodilla, longan, mamey sapote, black sapote ("chocolate pudding fruit"), miracle fruit, jaboticaba, cecropia ("snake fingers") and coffee beans, all of which can be sampled for free at the famous Redland Fruit and Spice Park, a local attraction.

Most of the country relinquishes fresh tomatoes in the winter, but not in South Florida where plentiful crops are seen, and Redland supplies them, along with a variety of winter squash and vegetables.

Redland is partially within and partially outside of Homestead, its general borders being (approximately) Southwest 137th Avenue on the east and west of Southwest 177th Avenue (also known as Krome Avenue) on the west. On the north it runs from just north of Coral Reef Drive (Southwest 152nd Street) to Southwest 288th Street on the south where it is congruent with Florida City.

Moving south again, past Florida City is what is today known as "the eighteen-mile stretch," which is Highway U.S. 1 between that city and the

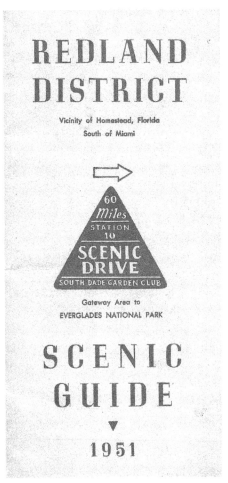

Left: A stunning *Redland District of Florida on the Lower East Coast* booklet published by the Redland District Chamber of Commerce.

Right: The 1951 Redland District's promotional booklet was less of a sales promotion and more of a tour guide, as noted by the title, *Scenic Guide/1951.*

Jewfish Creek bridge, which crosses that body of water (really a river) onto Key Largo. Until the end of service on the Florida East Coast Railway following the September 2, 1935 hurricane, the FEC's timetables showed four flag stops (places at which waiting passengers could signal the engineer to stop by "flagging" or signaling the train). Those four stations were, in descending order below Florida City, Wooddall, Glades, Cross Key and

Jewfish. Any place in a timetable at which a train was to stop, either by schedule or by flag, was deemed a "station," but unless there was a physical facility with passenger accommodations, the "station" was not a depot, and none of the four, used almost exclusively by fishermen and hunters, was anything even nearly resembling a depot, they having nothing other than a gravel base next to the track where the boarding or detraining passengers could stand and "flag" the train.

Even though in Monroe (not Miami-Dade) County, many consider Key Largo to be the southernmost point of the Homestead standard metropolitan statistical area and Key Largo-ites regularly make the trek from there to Homestead to shop, dine and enjoy various entertainment venues not available on the island.

The 1948 film *Key Largo*, starring Edward G. Robinson, Lauren Bacall and Humphrey Bogart, was set there, and the 1981 hit single "Key Largo" by Bertie Higgins was inspired by that film. With a 2010 population of 10,433, Key Largo is one of the largest islands in terms of population in the Florida Keys.

Chapter 10

TAKING HOMESTEAD INTO THE FUTURE

There are few things in life more exciting than a great comeback. Whether in team or individual sports, business or even government, what could be more exciting than to see a person or a group or an entity "coming back to life," overcoming enormous adversity, battling back against almost insurmountable and near-overwhelming forces and, in the end, triumphing? It doesn't get much better than that.

Combined, your co-authors have been a part of Greater Miami for more than 115 years. We have seen ethics triumph over corruption, right win out over wrong, good prevail over evil and light banish darkness, but never have we seen anything comparable to the comeback of Homestead following each of its setbacks, and those words never truer than after Hurricane Andrew.

It can best be said that the city, like a phoenix rising from the ashes, struggled, clawed and persevered its way back to a position of strength, and it has been that resiliency, that incredible willingness to fight its way back following each near-knockout and each battle against overwhelmingly difficult odds that has made and will continue to make Homestead the incredible and very special place that is has always been and will always be. "Everybody loves a winner," goes the saying, and Homestead, dear readers, is not just a winner but a winner with élan, class, graciousness and grace, a can-do attitude and a spirit of strength and belief in itself, its people and its future that is rarely seen in any sector of business or government, public or private.

There are, indeed, some very special people, groups and entities, both business and private-sector, that are and will be taking Homestead into that

Homestead's mayor Steven C. Bateman, reelected in November 2011 for a two-year term, served as mayor of Homestead during the city's centennial year.

great future, and the purpose of this chapter is to tell their stories and share with our readers some of what they have done as well as what they are doing to help build a greater Homestead.

The agricultural roots of Homestead are literal as well as figurative, and today's Dade County Farm Bureau, the first county farm bureau chartered in Florida, embraces that heritage even as it looks to the future. Originally organized in 1942 to bring growers together to collectively solve problems that they all faced, the first office in Homestead was opened in 1947. The move to the current building was in 1968. Renovated and expanded in 1984, it is the hub for activities that involve multi-generation agricultural families as well as newcomers, from global suppliers of produce and ornamental flowers and plants to produce stands by the road.

In looking across the business spectrum, however, no city or region can be successful without an active chamber of commerce, and Homestead certainly has that. The Greater Homestead/Florida City Chamber of Commerce, headquartered at 455 North Flagler Avenue in Homestead, is headed by Executive Director Rosa Brito. With over 450 members, networking events each month and ten committees, the chamber is a major partner as well as part and parcel of business success and exposure to

Homestead Then and Now is the wonderful booklet published by the city to present a view of the old and the new in Homestead.

the local market and is active in working to bring new businesses to the Homestead/Florida City area.

Homegrown banks are always very important to a community, giving a sense of having an anchor and a commitment to funding and supporting local businesses. Although banks of all types can be found throughout the Homestead area today, Homestead has been extremely fortunate in having two community-based banks that have sustained and grown through the

A beautiful ten-page booklet put together by the City of Homestead's Public Information Office extols the virtues of living, working and going to school in Homestead.

years. As a reminder, First National Bank of South Florida was founded in 1932 by Max Losner and a group of visionary businessmen who sought to charter a bank that would, initially, serve Homestead and Florida City. Year after year, the bank continued to grow and expand to new locations, and in 2001, the name of the bank was changed from First National Bank of Homestead to First National Bank of South Florida in order to more accurately reflect its market area and customer base.

The second of the locally based financial institutions is Community Bank of Florida (which began as Community Bank of Homestead but which has experienced such incredible growth, with offices south to Tavernier and into Polk County, close to Florida's west coast, that the name change necessitated by that growth became effective in 1999), the idea for which originated in February 1972. Beginning operations in 1973, the bank, with Robert Talley as its first president, has, under current president Robert L. Epling, been recognized statewide for excellence in banking and for service to the community.

And in speaking of rising from destruction, one must look to the base. Despite being closed by the air force after Hurricane Andrew, the Homestead Air Reserve Base, rebuilt in 1994, is becoming more and more active. It is now home to the 482nd Fighter Wing (FW) assigned to the Air Force Reserve Command 10th Air Force. The 482nd FW is a fully combat-ready unit capable of providing F-16C multipurpose fighter aircraft, along with mission-ready pilots and support personnel, for short-notice worldwide deployment. The wing has more than 1,500 members, including approximately 1,200 reservists, of which 250 are full-time reservists, in addition to 300 full-time civilians.

Besides the 482nd FW, there are other military tenants on the base, including Headquarters, U.S. Special Operations Command South (SOCSOUTH), the special operations component of U.S. Southern Command, Detachment 1 of the 125th Fighter Wing, Florida Air National Guard, the 50th Area Support Group, Florida Army National Guard, U.S. Coast Guard Maritime Safety and Security Team Miami, U.S. Army Corps of Engineers and the U.S. Customs and Border Protection's Miami Air Branch, whose aircraft conduct drug enforcement air interdiction missions from Homestead ARB.

During the Atlantic hurricane season, the 482nd FW routinely supports forward deployment of the Air Force Reserve's 403rd Wing from Keesler AFB, Mississippi, flying the WC-130 Hercules aircraft in the "Hurricane Hunters" weather reconnaissance missions. They have also hosted joint relief operations with the Federal Emergency Management Agency (FEMA).

"Flying High," a formation flown by the Black Diamond Jet Team, at the Wings Over Homestead air show on November 4, 2012. *Courtesy Michael A. Downs.*

In October 2005, Homestead Air Reserve Base teamed up with the Federal Emergency Management Agency to bring more than one million tons of relief supplies to South Floridians recovering from Hurricane Wilma.

While talk of and rumors regarding the base's full return to active status persist, only time will tell, but until then, Homestead Air Reserve Base is playing a vital and active role in the region's view to the future.

Indeed, as has been shown in this book, Homestead and the surrounding communities have always had close ties to the military. Those who stroll in Losner Park in downtown Homestead on Krome Avenue sometimes pause at the memorial stone next to the historic Seminole Theater. The stone pays tribute to fallen veterans, and there is a small plaza around the stone featuring bricks that are inscribed with the names of other men and women who have served in the military.

And what is a thriving community without healthcare? Fortunately, Homestead is blessed with a great hospital bearing its name. Homestead Hospital has been an important cornerstone of the south Miami-Dade community since 1940, when local physician James Archer Smith opened it as a ten-bed facility west of Krome Avenue.

Above: As up-to-date as it is beautiful, Homestead Hospital is nationally renowned by the AARP as one of America's "66 Safest Hospitals."

Left: Homestead Hospital is overseen by its CEO, Bill Duquette.

Today, Homestead Hospital is a modern, full-service 142-bed facility that opened in May 2007. The hospital brings cutting-edge technology and medical care to a fast-growing and traditionally underserved population. The hospital's emergency room, which cared for more than 85,000 patients in 2012, is double the size of the old one with forty-four private treatment rooms. There are, of course, numerous other areas, facilities and departments within the hospital, which has more than 1,300 employees and a staff that represents more than thirty-five countries and who speak more than a dozen languages.

Perhaps most important in terms of Homestead Hospital's already outstanding reputation is the fact that the April–May 2013 issue of its monthly publication, *AARP The Magazine*, published by the American Association of Retired Persons, named Homestead Hospital, in an article titled *Top Hospitals for Safety*, one of America's sixty-six safest hospitals.

There are, of course, many businesses that make Homestead the vibrant place that it is, and while it is simply not possibly to list all of them, let us mention a particularly unique and a well-established pair that residents and visitors alike enjoy: the Schnebly Winery and Brewery, the southernmost winery and brewery in the United States. On Southwest 217th Avenue, the winery presents wines crafted from tropical fruits and is available for tastings seven days a week. And on Southwest 216th Street is Burr's Berry Farm, run by Rob Burr and his brother. Rob participates actively in helping to not only "grow" Homestead but in adding to the enjoyment of being there through his annual January "Redland Riot Road Rallye" wherein participants follow clues to reach a final destination with those completing the rally enjoying an afternoon of friendship, fellowship and prizes.

In any discussion of Homestead's future, education is in the fore. Homestead is home to four high schools, with a fifth recently approved. Homestead's Medical Academy for Science and Technology (MAST) Academy is now rated third in the country in math, a singular honor. Miami-Dade College, at the urging of the late Homestead mayor Irving Peskoe and his wife, Bea, opened their Homestead campus more than twenty years ago. That campus is also one of the venues for the Homestead Center for the Arts, which offers the Bea Peskoe Lecture Series during the fall and winter as well as a series of community concerts and other events of interest to the greater community.

Finally and in closing, two venues in Florida City do need to be noted for they are an integral part of the area's future and have been an important part of its past. First, the Florida Pioneer Museum is an absolutely outstanding museum dedicated to South Florida history. The museum, on Krome Avenue just south of Lucy Street, is located in the former FEC Railway section foreman's home. Its large rooms and spacious porches lend themselves to giving the visitor a feeling of warm recall as he or she enjoys the unhurried atmosphere of a bygone era. While there are numerous eating places of all variety with an almost unlimited range of food for all tastes, the Capri Restaurant on Krome Avenue, several blocks from the Pioneer Museum, has been a local fixture since it was opened by Richard Accursio on July 27,

Robert Burr and Kathy Burr Magee are shown at Burr's Berry Farm just before the start of a recent Redland Riot Road Rallye.

Peter Schnebly and Denisse Serge-Schnebly have created America's southernmost winery and brewery, shown here in a beautiful nighttime image.

The Capri Restaurant on Krome Avenue in 1959, one year after it opened. *Courtesy Accursio family.*

A final look at our past as Florida East Coast Railway diesel 661 rolls by the Homestead depot on October 8, 1975. *Courtesy Richard Beall.*

With an equally important look at our future, a huge C-17 cargo plane lands at Homestead Air Reserve Base. *Courtesy Chris Green.*

1958, and it is believed that it is the oldest continually operating restaurant under its original management in South Dade County south of Shorty's Bar-B-Q near Dadeland. The meeting place of the Kiwanis and Rotary Clubs and the Redlands Woman's Club, the restaurant's commitment to serving the people of Homestead and Florida City is so strong that management had it reopened following Hurricane Andrew by late September, barely a month after the storm.

While it would be easy to write that the story of Homestead is now complete, the truth is that, like any great city, it is not now and never will be complete. Yet, as the city celebrates the exceptional milestone of its 100th year as Miami-Dade County's second incorporated municipality, the coming growth and the ongoing and never-ending renewal—all for the better—will continue to place Homestead in the absolute upper echelon of the most superior of American cities.

May the blessings of great residents, great businesses and great government continue to shine on Homestead and its friends and neighbors for at least another one hundred years.

ABOUT THE AUTHORS

Bob Jensen retired in Homestead as a navy commander after serving twenty-eight years. He served in Germany, the Philippines, at the U.S. Embassy in Cyprus and Iceland and twice at the National Security Agency and at Naval Security Group Headquarters in Washington, D.C.

He and his wife, Meda, have been married fifty-five years and are parents to four children and grandparents to three. After retiring from the navy, Bob became an officer of the 1st National Bank of South Florida and currently serves as vice-president for community liaison. He has served on the Miami-Dade County Historic Preservation Board and currently serves on the County Cultural Affairs Council. He is the longtime president of the Florida Pioneer Museum and has served as the chamber of commerce chair and chair of the chamber's Military Affairs Committee. Meda and Bob travel extensively every year but are always pleased to return home to Homestead.

Professor Seth H. Bramson is America's single most-published Florida history book author, with sixteen of his twenty-two books dealing directly with the villages, towns, cities, counties, people and businesses of the South Florida Gold Coast.

He is the company historian of the Florida East Coast Railway—the only person in the country who bears that title with an American railroad—and his book *Speedway to Sunshine* is the official history of that famous line. His collection of FEC Railway and Florida transportation memorabilia is the largest in the world: it is larger than the State Museum's collection and larger than the Flagler Museum's collection.

A graduate of Cornell University's famed School of Hotel Administration, he holds masters degrees from St. Thomas University and Florida International University, both in Miami. He is adjunct professor of history and historian in residence at Barry University and adjunct professor of history at FIU, where he teaches all of the university's south Florida and Florida history courses. In addition, he is historian in residence at FIU's Osher Lifelong Learning Institute and is adjunct professor of history at Nova-Southeastern University.

A Greater Miami resident since 1946, he is the founder of the Miami Memorabilia Collectors Club, and his collection of Miami memorabilia and Floridiana is the largest in private hands in the country.

Seth and Myrna have been married for thirty-seven years.

Printed in the USA
CPSIA information can be obtained
at www.ICGtesting.com
LVHW021940120923
757976LV00006B/69